One man's story is everyone's s
hand may not describe your ent
find places where you will nod your head and find yourself saying
"me too". It's for those "me too" junctures that this book was written. If you're in a place in your life that you need freedom and
deliverance you can say "me too" and if you just need to celebrate
and rejoice you too can say "me too". You will laugh, you will cry,
you will say "me too".

– Dr. Samuel R. Chand, Author of *Who's Holding*
Your Ladder? (www.samchand.com)

William M. Blackshear is the exemplification of never giving up
in spite of your circumstances. He has embodied the expression
"God will turn it around". He has overcome challenges throughout
his life that could have crippled him or left him lifeless - mentally,
emotionally, or physically - had he succumb to them. His innate
survival skills coupled with God's grace and mercy maintained
him, until such a time as he was ready to submit with his whole
heart to Christ by taking up his cross and following Him.

– Monica Burrell, MA., Director of Counseling
New Beginnings Church

From HELL to Grace

By

WILLIAM M. BLACKSHEAR

Restoration Consulting, LLC ◊ Charlotte, North Carolina

From Hell to Grace

Restoration Consulting, LLC
Southpark Towers
6000 Fairview Road, Suite 1200
Charlotte, North Carolina 28210

Project Restoration, Inc
PO Box 690248
Charlotte, North Carolina 28227

Disclaimer: I have tried to recreate events, locales, and conversations from my memories of them. In order to protect
the privacy of individuals, I have changed some identifying
characteristics and details, such as names, physical proper-
ties, occupations, and places of residence.

This book is not intended as a substitute for the medical
advice of physicians. The reader should regularly consult a
physician in matters relating to his or her health and par-
ticularly with respect to any symptoms that may require diagnosis or medical attention.

ISBN: 1481174827
ISBN 13: 9781481174824

From Hell To Grace

By William M. Blackshear

Restoration Consulting, LLC
Charlotte, North Carolina

TABLE OF CONTENTS

ACKNOWLEDGEMENTS. I
THE DEVIL INVADED MY HOME 1
KILL, STEAL, AND DESTROY. 11
THROUGH THE FIRE 21
STREET LIFE 27
JOY AND PAIN 35
NEW DOG, OLD TRICKS 45
IT'S GETTING CRAZY 53
NEW LOVE 59
DRIVER 63
WHAT'S BEEF? 71
GOD BLOCKED IT 75
ESCAPE FROM NEW YORK 81
NEW TRICK CITY. 85
BALLIN' AND SHOT CALLIN' 91
HEARTBREAKER. 97
MARRIAGE 101 103
SELF-RELIANCE 113
TRYING TO FLY STRAIGHT. 117
I STOPPED CALLING AND HE DIED 125
SOULED OUT 131
BLIND LEADING THE BLIND 137
FREE 149
AN OPEN LETTER 159
AFTERWORD 161
REFERENCES 165
ABOUT THE AUTHOR 167
RESOURCES 169

ACKNOWLEDGEMENTS

First and foremost, I thank my Lord and Savior Jesus Christ for saving me, pulling me out of hell, and moving me to grace. He knew the right people to bring into my life at the right time. Always remember to put your trust in God, no matter what you've been through. God loves us no matter what sins we've committed. When you repent of your sins and ask Him to come into your life, He comes with open arms and wipes away all of your sins.

Throughout my entire life I have experienced challenges with reading and writing as a result of living with dyslexia. However, this book you are about to read proves that if you put your trust in God, He will see you through. For every trial I experienced, one thing remained constant – praise, worship, and prayer. I am truly a worshipper.

I thank my church family at New Beginnings Church, especially my Pastor, Rev. Dr. Michael L. Henderson, Sr., and his wife, Rev. Twanna Henderson. Thank you for standing by me and believing in me, even when I messed up. I'll be the first to admit that when I joined the church and became a minister, I made some mistakes. I thank God that through the Holy Spirit that lives within you, both of you believed in me. I also thank my fellow armor bearers for their prayers and support.

I thank Minister Damian Johnson, for continuing to encourage me.

I thank Minister Randall Fisher, for being a true friend to me.

A special thank you to my mentor, Minister Kevin Moore, for your spiritual wisdom, guidance, and friendship.

I also thank the late Reverend Alan Brown, who told me in my youth that I would be somebody. No matter what he heard about me, he always believed in me.

I thank the Mecklenburg County Sheriff's Office for allowing me to work within their department, despite my background. I am especially grateful to Keith Cradle of the Adolescent Programs Division and Karen Simon of the Department of Inmate Programs.

I strongly believe in the good work being done with the youth in the Charlotte Metropolitan area.

I acknowledge Another Choice for Black Children's director, Ruth Amerson, for supporting me.

I thank Minister Rose Ling, for being the first person to review this book and for sharing your honest feedback.

A special thank you to my editor, Nicole P. Bell, of Alpha Omega Writing and Editing Services. I thank you not only for your expertise in editing, but also for having the spiritual eyes to help me prepare this book. You truly exceeded my expectations on this project. Thank you for allowing God to guide you!

Thank you Dr. Samuel R. Chand. It was a pleasure serving you when you spoke at my church. Thank you for being a man of your word and for providing honest feedback on my manuscript. Thank you for endorsing this book.

Thank you to the Jefferson family of Utica, NY, especially Jerald Jefferson, Jr., for being a second family to me and for taking me off the street when I was a young kid with nowhere else to go.

Thank you to the rest of my friends I grew up with, especially Mark Brooks and Brian Patterson.

There was a time as a minister that I was going through several difficulties and I felt like I wanted to just give up. I give a special acknowledgement to Minister Willette Robinson and her daughter, Minister Donteia Robinson. God used both of you at the right time. I thank you for believing in me when it seemed that everyone else had turned their backs on me.

I also want to thank Minister Christina Lee for encouraging me by allowing me to watch how God has used her as a public speaker.

I thank Trina Fullard, of McLeod Center, for allowing me to help teenagers in Charlotte, NC. You inspired me and encouraged me to do God's work with the children. Working at the McLeod Center enabled me to deal with issues that I had buried for years. It was the first place that God allowed me to use my gifts to help His children and to help myself.

I thank God for my family considering me an outcast. It made me strive to become the man that I am today. I am saved, on fire for God, and full of His Spirit. I thank God for the restoration of my family, especially my Mom and her husband, Mr. Smith. While writing this book, I realized that being a parent is tough when you don't have God in your life. I pray that one day all dysfunctional families will repent, reconcile, and recognize that the only way to heal is God's way—through love, grace, and forgiveness.

A special thank you to Joyce Meyers, for sharing your story of the abuse and neglect you went through as a child. Your materials helped me during my healing process.

I thank God for blessing me with my son, Daeon, who lives in New York.

I thank all my clients from *Project Restoration, Inc.* for allowing me to work with their sons. I am especially thankful for Daelen Bows, the one who was determined to exceed my expectations. I thank God for placing this young man in my life and for giving me the opportunity to experience the love and understanding that come from inspiring him to be successful. Through him, God has given me a second chance to experience raising a son.

A very special thanks goes to my best friend, for allowing God to lead her without any hidden motives. When I told her my story, she did not run, she did not leave me, and she did not judge me. She came to me and simply said, "I will help you finish your book." I thank God for bringing me through two failed marriages. He revealed to me, through prayer and fasting, that He was going to send me one woman to restore all that I thought I had lost. I thank God for showing me through our friendship and our continued work together on this book that you will one day be my wife. The best is yet to come!

If I have forgotten to mention anyone by name, please trust it is by fault of my mind, but certainly not my heart.

• • •

"Who shall separate us from the love of Christ? Shall tribulation, or distress, or persecution, or famine, or nakedness, or peril or sword? As it is written: 'For Your sake we are killed all day long; We are accounted as sheep for the slaughter.' Yet in all these things we are more than conquerors through Him who loved us. For I am persuaded that neither death nor life, nor angels nor principalities nor powers, nor things present nor things to come, nor height nor depth, nor any other created thing, shall be able to separate us from the love of God which is in Christ Jesus our Lord" (Romans 8:35–39 NKJV).

Chapter 1

THE DEVIL INVADED MY HOME

*"But God has chosen the foolish things of the world
to put to shame the wise, and God has chosen the
weak things of the world to put to shame the things
which are mighty"(1 Corinthians 1:27 NKJV).*

The funny thing about being born into this world is the challenges one must face. Some of us are faced with challenges at an early age, and I know that just like me, some of you wondered why. The Bible tells us that God knew us before we were born, and that He formed us in our mother's womb.[1] Satan, the father of lies, knows God's promises for His children; therefore, he knows that God has plans for us.

Satan wasted no time sending out his army to attack me. He used my family, especially my father. For those of you who don't know, Satan will always use someone you love, someone who is close to you. He knows that you will drop your guard with someone you love. If your loved one is not saved, it only makes it easier for the enemy to use him or her.

I refer to my childhood home as 'The Hell Pit.' Between the ages of two to four, my father rejected me. His friends paid attention to me and he didn't like it. When his friends came by to visit, they would ask, "Where's William?" and then they would pick me up and play with me.

We lived in the projects and one of my father's friends lived right across the hall. One day, he wanted to take me across the hall with him. He and my father argued about it. I could understand if my father was angry because he loved me and wanted to protect me, but that was not the case. He didn't love me and he didn't want anyone else to love me. There was a silent rivalry between my father and his friend. My father could not understand why his friend came to our house and asked for me. The attention was on me and not on him and that made him angry. After that day, whenever his friend came over, he told me to go lie down or take a nap, and he told him that I was sleeping.

My dad didn't even want my Mom to love me. I was really attached to my Mom and my dad didn't like the attention she gave me. Sometimes when she left the house, I was sad. When my father saw me crying, he yelled at me, and that drove fear into me. Instead of crying, I developed ways to hold back my tears but I never allowed his intimidation to discourage me from being around my Mom.

Sometimes, when I followed her around the house, I could see the anger in his eyes. However, when my Mom looked at him, he pretended that everything was all right and played around with me. I would be happy and afraid at the same time, because the minute my Mom left the house, his whole demeanor changed. He would grab me and say, "What did I tell you?" Then BOOM—I became a punching bag. Sometimes he slapped me so hard across the face that I fell down.

After he finished slapping me around, he sent me to the shoe closet. He made me stay in there for hours, sitting on the shoes and boots. My body became numb from sitting, but I was so scared that I made my body adjust to the pain and numbness. I was in there for at least three hours. At first, I thought he'd forgotten about me, but the truth was that he had taken a nap. While he slept, I sat in the closet, afraid to come out. By the time he told me to come out of the closet, I could barely stand up. My legs were so numb that I couldn't feel them.

When my Mom came home I got excited, but he made me seem like the worst kid out of the eight of us. He lied and told her that I had stood there and peed on myself and that I was in the room making a lot of noise, so he had to put me into the closet. What she didn't know was that I had been in there for three hours or more with nothing to eat. I went to bed sad and confused.

When I was in school, I had several nicknames. One was 'Greedy.' The kids didn't know that I wasn't eating at home, so I didn't mind begging for the food off their trays. One day, I walked by a dumpster at school and saw bread that was tossed away by the cafeteria. I took about three or four rolls and stuffed them into my pockets. I really didn't care about what people thought. I was hungry and I was preparing myself, just in case I wasn't going to be able to eat supper.

My dad was a towering two hundred and fifty pounds. When he screamed at me, I was terrified. The sound of his voice made me jump. I was eight-years-old and only weighed about fifty pounds. I was always on edge because I never knew what he was going to do. Eventually, I stopped crying because that always made it worse. I learned to hide my emotions but I was traumatized.

One time, my brother did something wrong and my father slapped him so hard that his head hit the doorknob and left a deep cut in the back of his head. There were times when my dad walked into the room and slapped me for no apparent reason. Then he would tell me to go to bed without eating. When my Mom came home and asked, "Why is William in the bed so early? Has he eaten anything?" My father lied and said, "He did something wrong." Honestly, I hadn't done anything.

The enemy (Satan) wanted to destroy my life early and quickly, because God put me on this earth for a special reason. The enemy's job was to kill me, steal from me, and destroy me, and he used my family to do it.[2]

. . .

When I was nine-years-old, my dad got a job doing construction work for Conrail. He was making good money, so we moved out of the projects. We moved into a big house, where my father's parents and his brother, my Uncle Harold, lived downstairs and we lived upstairs.

Before we moved out of the projects, I did one thing that gave Satan another point. I stole a pack of cupcakes from the store. I got away with it, but for the life of me, I did not understand why I took it. I guess I wanted it and didn't have the money for it, so I stole it. I was too young to realize that the enemy was testing me and planning for my future.

After we moved into our house and settled in, the enemy really turned up the heat. I was in the fourth grade when I discovered I had trouble reading, writing, and understanding my work. I tried to focus but I couldn't because there were so many things on my mind. I constantly lost focus because of the abuse going on in my home. I was afraid to be wrong, for fear of getting another beating with the ironing cord. When I was in class, all I thought about was what was taking place at home. When it was time for me to finish my work, so much fear and confusion was in me that I never completed it.

One week, my teacher gave me writing assignments to take home, but when I got home and tried to do my homework, I was too scared to even try to complete it. I feared that my father would come into the kitchen when I was doing my work. My father knew I had a problem with writing, so he made me do my homework in front of him. Each time I misspelled a word or formed a letter incorrectly, he beat me with a belt or an ironing cord, or he hit my hands with a thick ruler. My hands were in so much pain that it felt like heat was going through them. This brutal treatment went on for several hours. Finally, when he saw that his method was not effective, he sent me to bed.

In addition to this abuse, he put me on punishment for the rest of that week. I had to stay in my room when I got home from school and he made me wait to eat supper after everyone else in the family had finished. I failed fourth grade and had to go to summer school. My punishment for failing was to stay in my room for the entire summer.

• • •

As the summer ended and the new academic year started, I was promoted to the fifth grade. This was when the enemy launched an attack on my mind and tried to destroy me.

My teacher, Mrs. Davis, was mean but I knew that she wanted the best from her students. She desired this so much that she even had some of us stay after class to get extra help. That extra help brought me pain and suffering.

One day, after staying very late at a tutoring session, I walked through the door and was greeted with a barrage of leather whistling through the air and landing all over my body. My father thought that I had stayed after school for something I had done wrong.

A week later, my teacher wanted me to help her during lunch. As a result, I came home late. My father was angry. He made me undress and he tied me to the bed and beat me with an ironing cord. That afternoon, I went back to school with welts all over my body. My classmates noticed them and asked me what happened. I lied and told them that I fell and got hurt on my way home for lunch.

My teacher noticed a black and blue mark on my arm, so she rolled up my sleeve and asked what happened. I told her that my dad beat me because I was late getting home for lunch. She ran out of the classroom crying but she didn't call the cops or anyone else. She was very good friends with my Uncle Joe, who was heavily involved in politics. She eventually told him but he never did anything about it because my dad was his brother. He simply covered it up to protect the family name.

As time went on, I began stealing. At school, we had 'Fun Fridays,' when students were allowed to bring toys and candy to school. My dad had taken my toys away from me, so I couldn't bring them to school. To make up for it, I stole bags of candy. Eventually, my classmates gave me a new nickname, 'Candy Man.'

Mrs. Davis knew I didn't receive an allowance from my parents and she begged me to stop stealing. She also knew about the abuse I received at home but she wouldn't report it, so she didn't report my stealing either. The enemy just loved that and I did, too.

Eventually, she thought I had stopped. What she didn't know was that I had just gotten smarter by not bringing the whole bag into the classroom. There were times when she was suspicious, but every time she questioned me, I defended myself by saying that some other kid in the school gave me the candy. Of course, my classmates vouched for me. They were getting all the candy.

One day, I finally pushed my teacher too far. She was upset because I kept clowning around and disrupting class while she was teaching. She called my house on a *Sunday* morning, just as I was getting ready for church! This angered my dad so much that he made me take off my church clothes. I didn't get a beating that time, but I had to go into the closet and sit on shoes for about eight hours. By then, I'd become used to the closet and my body had adjusted to the pain.

The next week, on the way to school, my brother and I stole some candy from the store near our house. The owner of the store was a friend of my parents and they had a credit account with him. To our surprise, he called our parents and told them that he was putting the candy we had stolen on their bill. When my brother and I walked into the house, our parents were sitting on the couch waiting for us. They made us take off our coats and empty our pockets. They didn't beat us but they said things to us that made me feel like they wished they didn't have any sons. Their words cut me deeply and haunted me for years. I honestly wished they had just beaten me. It would have hurt less. I went to bed that night feeling lonely and depressed.

My attitude got worse, and so did my stealing. I was stealing candy every day. One day in class, I stole a classmate's money off her desk. That afternoon, the teacher found out that it was missing and told everyone we had to stay after school until it was either found or until someone confessed. I was nervous but I was not going to own up to it. The teacher made everyone walk around a desk with a hat on top of it and had everyone put his or her hands in it to place the money inside. I went first because she was aware of my punishment if I came home late. She knew I had it but she couldn't prove it. I left school that afternoon and went straight to the store and bought candy and chips with the money I'd stolen. When I got home, I told my parents that we had a party at school. To my surprise, they didn't question my story or call my teacher to make sure I was telling the truth.

• • •

Toward the end of the school year, the enemy tried to take me out again. I had a huge Afro, and one day I started scratching the side of my head. Then I started scratching all day, then all week. Finally, my teacher asked me to come to her desk so she could look at my head. She discovered I had ringworm on my scalp. I was sent home from school immediately because the school was afraid that the ringworm was contagious.

My Mom took me to the doctor and they said that all my hair had to be cut off. The Afro had hidden the ringworm. By the time they discovered it, it was sinking into the skin of my scalp. I was out of school for two weeks. I still have the scar.

I wasn't too happy about losing my hair because I had 'good hair.' It was wavy and when it was braided, it reached down the middle of my back. My paternal grandparents were part Native American and my grandmother had hair that grew past the middle of her back. My dad had beautiful hair, too.

While I was at home from school, I thought that maybe my dad and I could be buddies since we were the only ones at home during the day. That wasn't the case. I had to stay in my room. There were times I didn't get out of bed until noon but I wasn't sleeping in. Many times, I was awake and ready to get out of bed, but instead I would just lie there. I wasn't allowed to get out of bed until my dad gave me permission. He was punishing me for catching ringworm. When it was time for me to go back to school, I had to wear a stocking cap because I had medicated cream plastered on my scalp and there were sores on my head.

The devil continued using my dad to instill a spirit of fear in me. My dad developed a new way of punishing me—not realizing that he was letting the devil in on another level.

One night, he told me to come and watch television with him. I thought, *wow, I didn't do everything right and he's getting ready to let me watch TV with him.* To my disappointment, it wasn't a TV program that I would enjoy watching. Instead, my dad made me watch scary movies like *The Exorcist* and *The Omen.* After watching these movies, he told me to go to my room and turn off all the lights, and then he made me stand there in the dark for a while. I didn't fully understand what he was doing but fear crept up in me and I was scared after watching those movies. One day, I was so scared that I peed in my clothes and he punished me in his usual way.

At ten-years-old, I was afraid to sleep at night. I feared that I wasn't going to be able to eat dinner. I feared being beaten. I feared not getting good grades in school. I feared being put in the closet. Most of all, I feared my dad. My mind was slipping away.

When I was in school, I prayed that everything would go well and I wouldn't have to stay after. I couldn't stay focused because I was so gripped by fear that I was too scared to even try to do my work. I kept thinking about the beatings I would get if I failed or did anything wrong.

The mind is a terrible thing to play with because it leaves room for the enemy to come in and set up shop, and that's exactly what happened. I started thinking about how to avoid the beatings. At times, I tried to study and put forth the effort to do my work, but no matter how much I tried, I still failed, so I started cheating. I made sure to sit by the straight 'A' student at test time. This went on for months and my grades went from 'F' to 'D' and even 'C.'

The beatings stopped for a while but the devil wasn't going to rest—my stealing got worse. One day I went to a store with one of my friends and stole a big bag of candy bars. That time, we were caught. The police came and an officer took us home. Luckily, my dad wasn't home; however, my Mom was there and she was mad. She grabbed me, stripped me naked, and beat me like an animal with the ironing cord. Ten minutes passed and she was still swinging. Fifteen minutes passed and when I thought it was over, she told my brothers to hold my arms so she could continue beating me. By the time she finished, I had welts all over my stomach, legs, arms, back, and feet. When I got off the bed, I could barely walk. She told me to get dressed and sent me to the shoe closet to stay until my father came home.

Finally, about two hours after the brutal whipping, my father arrived. My mother relayed the incident to him. He ordered me to come out of the closet and take off my clothes so he could see the bruises. I knew that if the bruises weren't to his satisfaction, he was going to beat me again. However, when he saw the marks all over my body, the expression on his face let me know how terrible my wounds were. He sent me to bed. I was relieved but I couldn't sleep because of the pain. My body was burning and blood was trickling out of the welts.

The next day, I went to school and saw my partner in crime. The first thing he wanted to know was if I'd gotten a beating. Of course my response was, "No." I had anticipated this question, so I purposely wore a long sleeve shirt to cover the bruises and welts. My worst nightmare was realized when my friend bragged that he didn't get a beating either. I was too ashamed to tell him the truth.

For a week, things were okay, but the following week, my father called me into his room and started slapping me around. After the fifth time I got up from the floor, he said to me, "I hope you don't think you got away with anything just because your mother beat you. Now it's my turn." He beat me with the ironing cord on top of the welts that were finally healing.

I went to school the next day filled with rage and anger. I shut down and couldn't do my schoolwork. My teacher rolled up my sleeves and saw the marks, but again, because of my Uncle Joe's political involvement, she didn't report it.

I didn't steal again for the rest of the school year. What can I say? I couldn't keep taking those beatings. My body could only take so much.

Chapter 2

KILL, STEAL, AND DESTROY

In the fall, I began my sixth grade year. It was time for the evil one to turn up the heat. I was tired of getting beatings, so I started cheating again. At first, I sat by the smartest kid in school but that quickly ended because my teacher caught on to my scheme. He noticed that the other kid and I always got the same scores on our tests, with the same right and wrong answers.

It was time for me to use my devilish mind. I wasn't saved, so I walked, talked, and thought as the enemy guided me. I would sit up all night with the devil trying to figure out how to succeed at my schemes.

One night, he gave me the most wonderful plan, one that I could not think up on my own. It was time for another level, an illegal level. It was either that or the ironing cord, and let's face it—I wasn't choosing the ironing cord. I couldn't keep taking the pain of an ironing cord hitting my body and causing welts and blood clots.

I learned to master cheating so well that my grades improved from 'Ds' to 'Bs.' My father was amazed. My teacher tried his best to catch me. What really felt good was no more pain from the ironing cord for a while, but my mind became more evil and wicked. I had insight that couldn't be stopped. I could sense when my teacher was going to try to catch me cheating, so that day I wouldn't cheat. I came up with a way to never get caught.

If I had to do it all again, I would tell you that cheating just makes you appear smarter. If you are reading this and you are cheating in school—STOP! It's not worth it.

Even though I received good grades on my tests, my teacher was puzzled that I couldn't read or write. I explained to him that my brother and sister were helping me study. That story worked for a while. The more my grades improved the less my teacher was convinced that it was due to my own abilities. He was determined to catch me. I had to rethink how to succeed without being caught.

What my teacher didn't know was that the alternative to succeeding was getting a beating. There were times when I studied and did my own work but when I concentrated, memories of beatings, not eating, and sleeping in closets crept into my thoughts. In my mind, I could hear the screams from the torture that was taking place in my house. Every time I thought about it, my entire body quivered. I started clowning around in class to avoid thinking about those things.

One day at school, I was called to the counselor's office. That's when I found out that I was being placed in a remedial reading class. Even though I cheated on my tests, I couldn't cheat when it came to reading and writing. I would read and turn the words around and pronounce them the way I saw them.

In addition to the recommendation for remedial classes, I met with a psychiatrist to evaluate my problems with my schoolwork. He gave me several tests to try to figure out what was wrong, but I just sat there and wouldn't talk to him. My dad had told me, "You'd better not say anything about what goes on in this house!" When I got home that night, my dad beat me because I went to the psychiatrist's office.

Eventually, I started stealing again. I was even taking orders in school. I was the man, the Candy Man. I was bringing home so much candy that I'd be set for days. Everything was great until the day I came home and my father was home. I had five bags of candy but I stashed them under the porch to ensure he didn't catch me.

Then later that evening, I snuck out the back door when I thought it was safe to bring the bags into the house.

That night, while everyone was watching television, I pretended to go to bed early, but I wanted to eat the candy. Within thirty minutes, my father smelled the candy coming from my room. I received another naked ironing cord beating. Every time I did it the devil's way, he made sure I was caught. I didn't have Christ in my life so I listened to every word from the enemy.

• • •

The end of the school year rolled around and I passed and moved on to seventh grade, where I kept the same pattern of cheating and stealing. My grades remained the same. I could always get As but I made sure I also got Bs and Cs to keep the attention off me.

During my eighth grade year, the enemy introduced me to the spirit of enticement through the pornographic movies my dad rented. It started out subtly because we had HBO, Cinemax, and The Movie Channel. Back then, you were nothing in the neighborhood unless you had all three channels. This spirit of enticement came into our house when my dad had one of his friends place a chip behind the cable box so we could receive all the channels—including the Playboy channel. Since my room was connected to the TV room, I could see the television, even when they shut the door. I left my door slightly ajar so I could see everything through the crack.

When I watched those enticing movies, I became all hot and bothered but I didn't know what to do about it. I was only thirteen-years-old. I looked at the cute girls and at the attractive teachers at school with lust. I got so hot and bothered that I exposed myself to some of the girls at school. They looked but they didn't tell. Even at that young age, the enemy showed me who would receive my perversion. Then one day, I learned how to masturbate. I did this four to five times throughout each day while I continued to sneak and watch the movies. I also started stealing Playboy magazines.

While my body was coming alive, my grades were getting worse. One day, my dad was upset because my grades started falling again, so he came up with the punishment of me going to bed without eating. There were times when I wouldn't eat for the entire weekend. Not only was I not allowed to eat at home but I also wasn't allowed to ask my family for food or tell anyone that I was hungry. I knew that if I did and my dad found out, he would beat me again and put me in the closet . . . or worse.

We lived in a two-story home with five bedrooms upstairs and five bedrooms downstairs. We lived upstairs and my grandparents and Uncle Harold lived downstairs. It was easy for them to hear what was going on in our house. My uncles knew what my dad was doing to me but they had no compassion. Instead, they used it to take advantage of me.

· · ·

On a cold winter Sunday, around five o'clock in the evening, when most men would be watching the football game, my Uncle Harold asked me to come downstairs. I knew he had heard my dad yelling at me and he knew I was hungry.

While we watched the game, he asked me if I wanted some cereal. I said, "Yes." I was so hungry that I don't even remember what kind of cereal it was. I was just happy to be eating. When I finished eating, he told me that he was going to tell my dad that I was begging for food. He knew what my dad would do if he found out. I started crying and begged him not to tell. He said he wouldn't tell on me if I gave him sexual favors. Then he sodomized me in my grandparents' living room.

My dad had given me one order, "If you go downstairs begging for anything, I will skin you alive." I couldn't tell my parents what my uncle had done to me because the enemy was using my dad against me. It made me feel like everything was my fault. It was my fault when I got into trouble. It was my fault that I was hungry. It was my fault because I ate the cereal when

14

he offered it to me and it was my fault for disobeying my dad's orders.

Today, it still sends me into a panic when someone says they are going to tell on me. I fear that I won't get a chance to tell my side of the story, and if I do, I fear that no one is going to believe me.

One afternoon, I was caught stealing and when the cops brought me home, no one was there except for my Uncle Harold. He talked to the cops and let them know that he would tell my dad what happened. He never told my dad but he roughed me up so he could take advantage of me sexually. He knew I wasn't going to tell because I had just been caught stealing. For months, every Friday or whenever he heard my dad beating me, he would look for me.

The molestation made me furious and I had murderous intent in my heart. I was disgusted every time it happened and it made me nauseous. When I went to school and my male teachers came near me, I panicked. My mind was completely gone.

Eventually, Uncle Harold got a girlfriend and the abuse stopped, but that wasn't the end for me. One of my cousins raped me and another molested me. It was no coincidence that they were brothers. They both did it just once. When they left my life, I stayed far away from all of them.

• • •

One night, I'd had enough of the beatings and abuse. I planned to kill my dad. I took a butcher knife and tried to wait until he fell asleep so I could stab him. I knew there was a God because He put me into a deep sleep that night. When I woke up in the morning I was full of sorrow because I still had the knife in my bed. I thought about killing him again but then the thought came to my mind to take the knife to school and rape someone.

The spirit of lust was within me and I thought I could do it like the men in the movies. My plan was to find a girl and use the knife to put fear into her and make her have sex with me, just like the women in the movies I watched. I was too young to know that you shouldn't force a woman to be with you. I was fourteen-years-old with a knife in my pants and the enemy was leading me to kill, steal, and destroy. I did exactly what the devil told me to do.

I took the knife to school but then I decided to skip class. That afternoon, I saw a woman raking her leaves. I took the knife out but I really didn't know what I was going to do. I just stood there looking at her and she hit me with her rake. I ran and within ten minutes, the cops picked me up. I had thrown the knife away but they brought me back to the woman's house and she immediately identified me. They took me to the station and beat me with nightsticks and phone books. I thank God for intervening. Getting beat by the police was better than catching a case for rape.

Later, the cops called my parents. My dad was at work so they escorted me home. My Mom told me to go to my room until my dad came home. I sat there trembling because I knew what was coming. I wished that the police had just kept me because the beating they had given me was nothing compared to what my dad was going to do. When he came home, he had my brother hold me down and he beat me until I couldn't walk. I went to bed covered with bruises and with blood seeping through my shirt.

The next morning, I couldn't move but that didn't matter. He beat me again before I went to school. My spirit was broken but my mind was intent on hurting someone. I put another knife in my pants and I started knocking on doors in the neighborhood until a woman let me into her house to use the phone. When I pulled out the knife, she pushed me out of her house.

The irony is that I was a virgin and I didn't even know what I was going to do. That's how I know I was being led by the devil. After the devil saw that tactic wasn't working, I never attempted to rape someone again. Praise the Lord. I made it through the rest of the school year without incident.

• • •

One hot summer afternoon, my parents were at work so I had a little freedom. By that time, my home was like a prison. I came home from school, ate supper, and went to my room. If I was permitted to go outside, it was only for an hour or two and then I came back in the house. My parents wouldn't allow us to go outside if they weren't home.

That day, my younger brother was boiling hotdogs on the stove when I ran through the house shouting, "Dad is coming!" My brother snatched the pot off the stove just as I bumped into him. The water splashed all over the side of his face and shoulder. My brother sat there in pain for two hours because we were too afraid to tell our dad. I put cream on him and that helped for a little while but he was in a lot of pain. Eventually, we told my dad what happened and we took him to the emergency room. He had second-degree burns. Because I was the one who bumped into him, my punishment was that I had to stay in my room for the entire summer.

When summer finally ended, I was excited about starting high school, but I was also scared and ashamed. I was scared because I really didn't know what to expect. I was ashamed because my dad punished me by not buying me any sneakers for school. I only had two pairs of pants and two shirts for the entire year. My Mom told him that he was wrong, but that didn't change his mind. To make it look like I had new clothes, I wore an old pair of my uncle's sneakers and painted them white.

On the first day of school, I was the joke of the entire school. It was three weeks before the laughing and joking stopped. To cover up the shame, I started wearing some of my Uncle Lonnie's dress clothes. I really liked Uncle Lonnie because he didn't like what my dad was doing to me. He took me out to eat and he let me wear his dress clothes. He never tried anything with me or made me do sexual favors for him.

Eventually, my dad loosened up and began letting my older brothers, my sisters, and me attend the dances at school and the college parties. This was a completely new arena for the devil to set me up for heartbreaks and setbacks.

It all started when I began wearing my uncle's clothes. I received a lot of attention from girls and that made me feel good because I liked the attention. However, there was one problem, my dad didn't believe in dating. Girls gave me their phone numbers, but I couldn't call because I wasn't allowed. I sneaked and called girls when my parents weren't home, but that wasn't often. Since talking on the phone was impossible, the girls lost interest and eventually passed me by. I started wanting something that my flesh couldn't have. Again, the devil had room to get in. I stole my sister's jewelry, took it to school, and gave it to my girlfriend.

One Saturday afternoon, my brother and I were preparing to go outside to play baseball when the phone rang. It was my dad. He told my Mom to tell me to go to my room and let the others go outside. Later, he came home and asked me, "Who is Yvette?" It surprised me that he knew the girl I called myself dating. Then he took out the bracelet and asked me where it came from. I told him I found it. He knew I was lying and sent me to bed without lunch or dinner. I had to stay in my room every day after school for a week and I wasn't allowed to watch television.

When I got to school on Monday, everyone was laughing because my so-called girlfriend, Yvette, had told them what happened. I felt so stupid. I told her I was going to beat her up but I never touched her. Some roughneck girls did it for me. They were jealous of her because she was short, light-skinned, and had long, pretty hair. For a while, I was the nerd and the laughing stock of the school.

Eventually, I wised up and stopped stealing things for girls, but that didn't stop them from liking me. I wasn't getting love from home, so when girls showed interest I would go all out to show them that I really liked them. Little did I know, I was pushing them away because I was coming on too strong.

During freshman year, my writing and reading grew worse. I had an IQ of forty at the time. I hid it well because I still sat by the smartest kid in class so I could cheat off his or her paper. I did this to avoid the beatings. My dad never understood that I had a learning disability. To him, I was just stupid and dumb. Eventually, I made it out of ninth grade but my self-esteem was low and all I could think about was revenge.

I wanted to get back at all the girls who had made me feel stupid. I tried being nice to them and they laughed at me. I learned quickly that girls don't like nice guys and so I decided to strike back. I was tired of being walked on and abused. I needed love. I had been raped, molested, and abused. I was enraged, depressed, empty, unloved, and out of my mind. I knew that feeling of revenge would stay with me. I still didn't know God or how to pray. Again, the enemy gave me a master plan.

I dreamed of going to high school and wearing name brand clothing. The plan was simple. I would go into the mall and steal my own clothes. I was tired of seeing my brothers and sisters dressing nice for school while I wore hand me downs that were too big for me. The plan was sweet. I would go to the mall, steal the clothes, and tell my parents that one of my friends gave me the clothes because he worked in the clothing store. The plan worked for a while, until my dad wanted to see if it was the truth. I told one of my best friends to call my house and tell my dad that he gave me the clothes. How many of you know he didn't do that favor for nothing? I had to steal for him, too, which I didn't mind. My dad never questioned me about it again.

I was the best-dressed kid in the entire school and I liked the attention. People in school asked me, "Can I wear that if you're not wearing it tomorrow?" and I would tell them, "Sure, but for a small fee, I can get you one of your own." I had a small business providing clothes for the kids in school. I had at least one hundred to two hundred dollars in my pocket each week.

Guess where the money went? Food. I went to Burger King every morning and ordered three breakfast sandwiches. Then, during second period, I skipped class, went back to Burger King, and ordered three more. Burger King became my hang out. I no longer ate lunch in school. I would have two Whoppers, a large fry, and a soda every day. I had so much money that I took kids from school out to lunch with me and told them to order whatever they wanted.

I was buying my own food—even for the house. I pretended I was making money by going house-to-house asking neighbors if they needed their driveway shoveled. My dad didn't mind this because sometimes he made me buy candy for my sisters with the money I made. I hated that because I hated them. I have five sisters and my parents favored them. They always got things, as if my brothers and I didn't exist. Even though I had money from stealing clothes, there were times I would come home and say that I couldn't find a single neighbor that would let me shovel, just to avoid buying my sisters anything. My dad made me hate them because he favored them so much. I even had to do their chores. I felt like a bastard child.

What took root in me was another spirit sent by the evil one—a spirit of hatred for women. Instead of loving my sisters, I envied them to the point of picking physical fights with them. I didn't care that they were girls. All I saw was that they were treated with love while I was being treated like a bastard child. I asked myself, *how can my parents not show me love or even tell me that they love me?* All I heard was that I was no good and that I would never be anything. Then another spirit attached itself to me—the spirit to fight and hit girls.

One day, I wanted to watch the Dallas Cowboys, my favorite team, and my sister wanted to watch her favorite show. As always, I didn't get to watch my team and she got to watch her show. I cursed her out, slapped her in her face, and pushed the television on the floor. When my dad came home, he beat me and I had to stay in my room without dinner.

Chapter 3

THROUGH THE FIRE

I continued to have challenges with my writing in school. My dad made me write in front of him and when I couldn't do it, he beat me on my knuckles with a two-by-four board from under the bed. That went on until my knuckles were so bruised and swollen that I couldn't clench my hands when I woke up in the morning. I couldn't write the way my dad wanted me to and he told me I was dumb and stupid. He loved beating me down with words that would later scar me for years.

Words are one of the devil's most powerful tools. He knows that if we hear positive words such as, "You're great" or "I love you" or "You're the best," or "You can achieve anything because you're smart," we will succeed in life. However, the enemy used my dad to say the opposite words to me and they haunted me for years. After all the beatings and punishment, my dad was still determined to break me down to nothing.

There were times when he made sure I did all the chores in the house. One day, there was a pile of dishes after a big holiday dinner and he said, "I don't want the girls to do the dishes. Let the dumb black kid do them." I was in the kitchen for at least an hour, cleaning the kitchen and washing all the dishes.

Later that night, around three o'clock in the morning, he woke me up to say they weren't done right. I woke up to feeling the ironing cord slash across my back. My dad weighed two hundred and sixty-five pounds then and the force of his swing hitting a ninety-eight pound kid with an ironing cord was like fire. The lashing made me yell with pain but then I got another lashing to keep quiet. In the end, I had to get up and do the dishes again.

The next morning, my dad told everybody to get up, except me. I had to stay in bed until everyone in the family finished breakfast. Then I was permitted to go in the kitchen and eat. My food was ice cold by then and I had to eat it without warming it up. Again, I had to wash all the dishes, in addition to completing my own chores. This made me so angry. I felt more like the devil every day. I was mean and hateful towards my dad and sisters because I felt it wasn't fair. Even though I knew my sisters had no control over it, I was mad because I was doing their chores. It was time for the enemy to try something new.

One summer day, I was playing ball at the park. Out of nowhere, this guy came running full speed at me. The next thing I knew, we were fighting and I didn't know why. We fell to the ground, my arm hit a piece of glass, and it went straight into my elbow. I went home and told my dad what happened and he said, "You shouldn't have been fighting." He told me to go to my room without even looking at my wounds. I couldn't tell my Mom because she was out of town.

At about two o'clock in the morning, my elbow was swollen and blood was all over my sheets. My elbow and forearm looked like three baseball bats put together. It stayed like this for five days until my Mom got home. After she looked at it, she took me to the emergency room. My arm and elbow were so infected that it took the doctor three hours to drain the fluid. The x-rays showed small pieces of glass in my elbow that needed to be removed but because the glass had stayed in my arm for five days, it had cut off pieces of my elbow bone. At the time, my parents didn't have insurance, so they couldn't remove the chips of glass from the bones in my elbow. Today, I have to be careful not to lift too much weight on my arm or rub it up against anything because the pain comes back in an awful way.

Even though I didn't start the fight, my dad never took the time to listen and find out what happened. I went to the hospital and created a bill he had to pay, and that was the reason he gave for not buying me any new school clothes.

I began my sophomore year with my clothes from the previous year. They were too tight and too small. On the first day of school, everyone in the classroom laughed at me. Even my teachers grinned and smirked about my sneakers being old and run down. As a result, more hate and anger rose up in me and I let the devil in again. I sat in the classroom thinking of how I could come to school and not look crazy. I couldn't wear my uncle's clothes anymore.

I started going to the mall again to steal my own clothes. I snuck the clothes in the house during school hours while my parents were at work. I told them that some of my friends gave them to me because they couldn't wear them anymore. My dad always accepted that because it meant that he didn't have to buy clothes for me. One day, I got in trouble in school and he made me put the new clothes in his room and wear my old ones again. I was so humiliated that I went on a stealing spree. I stole clothes and left them at my friend's house. I went to his house in the morning before school and changed my clothes. I also stole food and candy and stored it in my room. I was at a point where I just didn't care about being caught anymore. The very thing I knew was wrong was exactly what I embraced. I said to myself, *what else do I have to believe in?*

It must have amused my dad to see me suffer, just to feel he was in power and in control. Little did he know that the only person who was in control was the enemy. The enemy was controlling him by making him harm me and the enemy was controlling me and making me steal. My dad even took things out of the refrigerator or stole my sister's jewelry and blamed me. Then he punished me by not feeding me and sending me to bed early.

One night, at around two o'clock in the morning when I was pretending to be asleep, I heard him creep into my room and throw a brown paper bag on the floor. I got out of bed, checked to see what was in the bag, and saw half a sandwich. Then I closed the bag and went back to sleep, wondering why he had thrown the bag in my room.

I received my answer the next morning when he got up and went into the kitchen. He yelled, "Who took my bag out of the refrigerator?" Then he came into my room with my brothers and demanded to know how the brown paper bag had gotten into my room. I was too afraid to say that I saw him throw it in my room, so I tensed up and started to cry. He told me to get out of bed and then he slapped me in the face. I fell to the floor. He told me to get up and slapped me down again. I wondered if my mother would come and save me, but once again, that didn't happen. Finally, after my face was sore and numb on one side, he told me to get back in the bed without breakfast, lunch, or dinner that day. It was a Saturday and it was hot outside. My brothers and sisters went outside to play while I was in the bed miserable and angry.

• • •

Some of the best times I had as a child were when I knew my dad was getting dressed to hang out with his friends. I felt like the warden was leaving and I got excited, but the minute I heard the key in the door, my heart dropped and the fun was over.

One hot, summer day I actually got the chance to be outside with my friends. We were sitting on the porch, laughing and cracking jokes, when my dad called me upstairs and said we were being too loud. He told me to go to my room and said, "You're dumb, black, and stupid." I cried because I believed him. In my mind, I thought it had to be true if my dad was the one saying it. He also said that he would never be caught in public with me because I would embarrass him, which he would never allow to happen. He never took me anywhere—not to a baseball game or a football game, not to go out to eat or even just for a ride in the car. I felt like something was wrong with me because we never went anywhere fun.

All I did was stay in the house and think about what I would love to do. Dreaming and wishing didn't cause me any pain. They were the things that my dad couldn't take from me. Even though what I was dreaming wasn't all godly, it was still my vision at the time and that's all that mattered. The funny thing is that I completed everything I dreamed about, even the things that were wrong. I later discovered that dreaming was a gift from God, despite the devil using it to make me think of things that were ungodly.

I daydreamed about women and being in relationships with women. It was time for a brand new way of looking at life. I became involved with any girl that paid me attention. This was the spirit of naïveté. All a girl had to do was tell me she liked me and I fell for her, not knowing that she was already in a relationship and just needed someone to make her boyfriend jealous. Boy, was I stupid!

The enemy used these tactics to allow a spirit of low self-esteem to come into my life. This spirit gripped me and made me feel worthless. My heart became cold and empty because I would given another person the one thing that God gave me to make a connection with Him—my heart. Once I allowed the wrong thing or person into my heart, I became like a zombie, walking around empty because of pain and heartache. I learned to hide my emotions, pretending that I was not hurt. In fact, I was wounded and depressed.

I had many girls come into my life and break my heart, but because I buried the hurt, I found myself in relationships that only brought more pain and heartache. To get over my pain, I increased my eating and stealing. Inside I was screaming for help, but I had learned to hide my emotions and to mask my pain.

I developed behavioral problems that manifested themselves as bipolar and paranoia. One minute I'd be up then the next I'd be down. There were times I was sick in school and my teacher sent me to the nurse. She told me I was too sick to go back to class but I would beg her not to send me home. I was too afraid that I would get in trouble and have to miss a meal because I came home for being sick. Usually, I just stayed in school vomiting and shaking.

There were times I was awakened in the middle of the night because my parents were arguing. I would go to school the next day tired and angry. I couldn't focus at all. There were days when we had testing and I fell asleep on the desk. Before I knew it, the dismissal bell rang. Of course, I failed the test. This went on throughout the school year.

• • •

One sunny Sunday afternoon, I noticed my Mom preparing to go to one of her friend's homes and I asked if I could go with her. She agreed but it caused a major problem. Not only did my dad not want me to go with my Mom, but he also didn't want her to leave. To my surprise, my dad slapped me so hard that I fell down the stairs. I still went with my Mom but I cried all the way to her friend's house. My body adjusted to the pain and misery but I often wondered why my parents were filled with so much hate. As time went on, cruelty became just another part of my childhood.

I started thinking I must be the worst kid in the world because all I got in my life were punishments and beatings. I have to admit that I caused some of the problems due to my stealing and mischief, but at other times, the abuse in the home was simply because my dad was just an angry man. I believe his anger came from his own upbringing. He was raised in a family with sixteen kids during the Great Depression. I know my grandfather had to have the highest level of discipline. He was trying to feed sixteen kids and make sure they all stayed in line.

My childhood was challenging because the enemy tried his best to take me out and disqualify me, but I have to believe that God was with me and that He is real. I can truly say that as I look over my life and realize that I made it out of the house of hell, it was all because the enemy came at me with his best shot, but God blocked it all. I may have bumps and bruises, but through it all, I'm still standing. I came out of the fire smoke free.

Chapter 4

STREET LIFE

It was well after midnight on a cold fall evening when I said to myself, *enough is enough.* My parents had company over so they were in the kitchen drinking and talking. I already had my bags packed with two sets of clothes. I threw them out the window, went to the door in the other part of the house, opened it slowly, and ran down the stairs to my freedom. I snatched my bags off the ground and ran like I was being chased by a wild pack of dogs.

When I finally made it to my friend Jerome's house, he wasn't home. I should have expected that. It was a Friday night and he had already graduated from high school. I decided to change my clothes and go to the club where I knew he would be.

When I arrived at the club I found Jerome, told him I needed to stay with him, and he said that it was cool. I wanted to dance but I felt like everyone knew I had run away from home, so I stayed to myself in the corner.

I woke up the next morning at Jerome's and ran to the super-market to steal breakfast. I stole sausage, bacon, eggs, and juice. Since I was not paying rent to my friend, I continued to steal breakfast and dinner. I'd go to the store and steal shrimp, fish, steaks, pork chops, and beef. Hey, I figured if I was going to steal, I might as well steal the best. I no longer lived at home and I felt free as a bird. Nonetheless, whenever I was out, I was looking over my shoulder to see if my dad's car was behind me.

When I went outside, I stayed away from where my parents lived. If they were looking for me, I never saw them. When I went to school, I was nervous because I didn't know if they would come to the school looking for me. I didn't have to worry about my brothers or sisters because I was the only one in high school at the time. My older siblings had already graduated and my younger brothers and sisters were still in middle school. It was challenging going to school because my parents' house was across the street from my high school. I missed several days of school because I was afraid I might run into my family and I would have to go back home.

After I left home, my stealing was out of control. Jerome and I wore the same size, so I stole clothes for the both of us. We would just switch off with our outfits. When we went to the club, we were the sharpest dressed guys in the place. I had one problem though. I didn't know how to approach women. I was lame. On the other hand, women loved me. They always approached me and told me I was handsome but I didn't know how to respond to them. Living a sheltered life didn't help me at all. I couldn't believe it—I was afraid of women. They told Jerome that they thought I was fine and handsome, but because I was very shy and timid, they assumed I was stuck up and conceited. The truth was that I just didn't know what to say to them.

Looking back, I realize that God allowed that to happen because I was still a virgin. I hadn't been with a woman yet. However, the more women approached me, the more curious I became. You know they say that curiosity killed the cat. Well, for me, it killed the holiness in me.

As the weeks went by, I started doing poorly in school. I stayed up all night with Jerome and it was hard for me to get up in the mornings for class. I was failing in all my subjects due to my frequent absences but I didn't care. I was having fun just hanging out with my friends.

When the weekends came around, I went to the club because I wanted to feel like another person. Before we went out, we always listened to music and drank beer and alcohol. The first time I tried pot, I choked trying to hold the smoke in my mouth. My friends showed me how to inhale and when I did that along with the alcohol, boy what a rush!

We went to the club and when we got there, all eyes were on us. There were five of us and we all stayed clean and decked out, thanks to me. However, I still didn't know how to relate to women. I just stood around and posed on the wall like I was a model. Women approached me and asked if I wanted to dance, but I often said no. I was afraid that I wouldn't know how to dance.

Eventually, I learned to dance by coming to the club every week and watching everyone. Once I learned, you couldn't keep me off the dance floor! I danced with women like I was making a music video. It drove them crazy and before I knew it, I had a name in the club. They called me 'Pretty Ricky' because I had a smooth baby face, dressed sharp, and kept my body in shape.

Women would ask Jerome for his home phone number so they could call and talk to him, but they were really hoping to talk to me. I wouldn't talk to just any girl. I was picky. If the girl wasn't beautiful to me—thick and fine—I told Jerome I didn't want to be bothered. He would say, "Blackshear, you're crazy!" Even when I met my type, I wouldn't talk to them if I knew they talked to certain guys. I knew the guys they talked to and I knew they were sleeping with everybody, and that immediately turned me off.

Now there were times when I was so high on drugs that I would give in to women and regret it when I woke up in the morning. I would think, *why did I even allow her in my bed?* The funny thing was that I never had sex with the women I brought home from the club because I didn't know what to do. They didn't care. Being next to me was all they cared about.

A month before my seventeenth birthday, I started renting X-rated movies so I could learn what to do. After I watched the movies, I believed I was ready, but when the time came, I was afraid.

Then one day, it happened. I had sex in the stairwell of an apartment complex. After that experience, I felt that I was ready for the next time a woman in the club asked to go home with me. I had allowed yet another spirit to come into my life—the spirit of lust. Sometimes the only reason I went to the club was to look for sex. My mind and body desired it often. When I couldn't get lucky, I went home and watched X-rated movies.

My friends often told me that it wasn't that I couldn't have someone, my problem was that if I didn't think the person suited my taste, I passed. I would size a woman up from head to toe and if I didn't feel it, I said no. My friends would get mad and call me stupid. They tried to persuade me to bring the women back to the house so that they could have them, but I refused. Sometimes there were women who were ten years older than me asking me to come home with them. However, only one type of woman was of interest to me, the classy type. The classy women turned me on. Their hair and nails would be done, they dressed nice, and the whole look made my entire body sing.

I was unaware that I was being introduced to an enticing spirit called seduction. This spirit knows how to make men and boys say yes instead of no. When it walks across the room, everything in your body is saying, "Who is that?" You fall into a daze with all types of thoughts going through your head. Your flesh takes over and it wants what it wants. The chase is on!

As the weeks and months passed, I ran the streets and my stealing habit spiraled out of control, but I had to survive. Every week, I took orders from my friends so I could have money to eat, to buy school clothes, and to buy street clothes. I took orders to steal baby clothes, suits, shoes, boots, jackets, women's clothes, and small appliances.

I still had a problem with stealing food even though I had money. I was in so much mental bondage that I thought I needed to hold on to my money and keep stealing food. I used the money for my weekend partying. I easily spent over a hundred dollars every weekend. My friends and I bought alcohol and drugs and we got higher than a kite! I also needed to keep up with my roommate. He had a construction job and was making good money. I didn't want to be left on the sideline broke. When Fridays came around, we pitched in and had a good time.

Eventually, the weed lost its affect, so we graduated to cocaine. Initially, I was nervous about it. The first time Jerome came home from work and said he had some 'coke,' I didn't know what it was. When he took it out, it was white like snow but it looked like flour. He told me to put it on my tongue and when I did, it numbed my entire mouth. Then he told me to put a little on my finger and sniff it. When I sniffed it, I didn't feel anything at first, but within minutes I felt like I had just drank two cups of straight, black coffee.

The pot we smoked and the liquor we drank made me feel like I was on cloud nine. I was mellow. Sometimes I was so high that I would forget where I was. When I sniffed cocaine it brought my weed high down but I still felt like dancing. By the time we got to the club, I wasn't that shy guy anymore. I asked women to dance and they were impressed that I stayed on the floor with them through four songs straight. They didn't know I was coked up and high on weed and alcohol. I was a brand new person. I liked it, and so did the women.

I was having fun and when the weekend ended, I didn't want to go to school. I felt like I was above the kids in my class. Furthermore, I still had a reading and writing problem. I went to school maybe three days a week, but I wouldn't do anything. I skipped classes. My mind was not focused on schoolwork. I was trying to catch up with what I felt I had been missing in my life.

• • •

One day I went to the mall to steal and it happened. As I was leaving the mall, two security guards stopped me. They escorted me back into the store and found everything I had. They called the cops and I was hauled off to jail. When I got to the station, I gave them a fake name. It worked until they had to call someone to verify that

I was who I said I was. Once they couldn't reach anyone they told me I had to stay until they could verify my identity. I finally broke down and told them my real name. After they verified who I was, I left with a scheduled court appearance and a ticket. When I went to court, I was ordered to do community service and pay a fine.

You would think this would have stopped me from stealing, but it didn't. Stealing was all I knew how to do to survive. My face was known at the mall, so when I went into the store the employees rushed up to me and asked if they could help me. I told them I was just looking and they would assign someone to follow me around the store. That still didn't stop me. I stole clothes right in front of them. I surprised myself. I had become a professional.

One Friday night, Jerome got mad because I wouldn't steal for him. When I got to his house, it was late and he wasn't home. The door was locked and that was the first time that had happened. That night, I wandered the streets, cold and hungry. I couldn't steal from the local store so I found food in the garbage. I checked cars in the parking lots for a place to sleep. I looked in one of the cars and I saw a man with a prostitute. I stuck around to watch, which only intensified my sexual appetite.

I slept in an unlocked car and when I awoke, I went back to my friend's house to see if I could get in. I arrived at the house with breakfast food and he was happy to let me in. When I got inside the house, he told me that he thought he would have seen me at the club. I told him that I couldn't get in the house and I didn't have the appropriate clothes to wear in the club. Since I wasn't paying rent and he and his family were letting me stay there, what could I say?

Later that evening we got high again on weed, alcohol, and cocaine. Then we went to the club, hit the dance floor, and danced all night long. After I left the club, I went back to the same parking lot and watched another prostitute in a car with a man.

On Sunday, we didn't have to worry about dinner because we ate at Jerome's parent's house and watched football (Dallas

Cowboys, of course). I enjoyed the family time because we never did that in my family. I knew Jerome felt bad about the previous night when he asked me where I slept. I lied and told him I had taken a girl home. I was too ashamed to tell him the truth.

The next Friday, Jerome's cousin had several food vouchers from the welfare department, so we took them to the store and tried to use them. We loaded up the shopping cart with food and approached the register. The total came to three hundred and twenty dollars. We gave the cashier the vouchers and before we knew it, we were being escorted to the back of the store by security guards. As we continued to the back of the store, we silently signaled to each other to run—Jerome went one way and I went another. To my surprise, the cops were already en route to pick us up. The cops rode up behind me, jumped out of their patrol car, and arrested me. My boy was already in the car.

When we arrived at the police station, we went into separate interrogation rooms. We both said that Jerome's cousin gave us the vouchers, which they already knew because they said they had been looking for him. We told them that we didn't know the vouchers were stolen. To our surprise, they believed us and let us go. Boy was God with us that day!

We arrived home shortly after midnight, so we got dressed and went to the club. By that time, my mind was going crazy. We had just left the police station after several hours of interrogation and minutes later we were at a nightclub. Time and life were going by so fast that I thought, *what just happened? What am I doing here?* My mind was stuck on the fact that we didn't go to jail. I couldn't believe it. God's grace was on my life.

Chapter 5

JOY AND PAIN

As I continued my search for significance, I met Renee, the girl next door. One night, Jerome and I knocked on her door and she let us in. Jerome told me to sit in the TV room while he went into the bedroom with her. After a while, I crept back to her bedroom door and opened it to see them having sex. I was sad because I thought she was a good person. I liked her but she was allowing herself to be used by him. I closed the door and went back to watching television. While I waited for Jerome, I saw her son outside playing and so I hung out with him throwing the football.

The following week, I went to Renee's house to see if her son could come out and play ball. She asked me if I wanted to come in and wait until he finished his homework. I agreed, because the truth was that I had been walking the street outside, waiting for Jerome to come home. Her invitation was a blessing. I ate dinner and I wasn't in the cold any more. It felt good being in a house where there was heat and hot water because at Jerome's house I was sleeping on a pull out sofa bed, the heat didn't work well, there was no hot water, and mice were running through the house.

I was comfortable with Renee. She fed me dinner and let me watch television with cable. Surprisingly, having sex with her wasn't on my mind. I regarded her as special. Yeah, I know what you're thinking—how stupid was I?

We started a relationship. I was eighteen-years-old. She was twenty-four and had a seven-year-old son. There was just one problem, I knew her son's father from church, but I didn't think it would make a difference because she wasn't married to him and she wasn't dating him anymore.

I started to really care for her and her son. We felt like a family and I needed that in my life. Even though she had other male friends and the situation was not favorable for me, I made it work so I could have a chance to feel wanted. I started staying over and watching her son while she went to work. I fooled myself into believing that I was getting over what took place in my childhood by creating a family with Renee and her son.

Everything settled down. I stopped hanging out with my friends. I stopped going to the club. I started feeling safe. I had somewhere to eat, somewhere to lay my head, and someone to talk to. The best part was building a friendship with her son. Nevertheless, I had one problem that continued to follow me—shoplifting. I brought home groceries, clothes, and household items without even having money. Renee didn't ask me where the stuff came from. I believe she already knew, but just like me, she enjoyed the company.

After several months, she came home one day and told me that she was pregnant. I was very excited but at the same time, I didn't know what to expect. She always told me that it didn't matter if we didn't have everything. She was just excited that I was there.

I didn't care what she told me. I was going to make sure that my kid had everything it needed. I was a professional at shoplifting and I knew I could make a big hit. The devil was crafty. After I made sure her son was fed and Renee was asleep, I started going out again with my boys. Eventually, we came up with a plan to rob the sneaker store in the mall.

We stole $30,000 worth of athletic gear. We had sneakers, sweatsuits, hats, and other items, but we agreed not to wear anything until everything died down. However, when you spend time with the devil long enough, one thing he knows are your likes and dislikes. One of my likes was dressing to impress.

One Friday evening, my high school basketball team was playing another team that was very popular. People came from all over for this game. I thought to myself, *I have to be clean for this one.* I dipped into the stash and pulled out a fresh sweat suit with matching sneakers, a nice hat, and designer shades. I was clean from head to toe. I walked into the basketball game and I heard people saying, "Oh my God. Look at Blackshear." The devil knew that's what I wanted to hear. Boy, I felt good. Girls were giving me their phone numbers and asking me where I got the clothes because they had never seen them before. You gotta understand, a new brand of sneakers was coming out and we took the entire stash before it could hit the shelves.

I started taking orders and telling people that I could hook them up for a fee. My life was all about money, clothes, and shoes. You couldn't tell me anything. One of my friends who broke into the place with me pulled me aside at the game and screamed, "Yo, that's tight! But didn't we say we were gonna chill?" Even though he was mad, he couldn't help noticing me.

The next day, all I could think about was how everybody's eyes were fixed on me, complimenting me. It made me feel like the man. I had money, which made me feel good because I used the money to do things around the house. Renee was coming along with the pregnancy but she was concerned because she saw all different types of clothes for her, her son, and me. I told her that I had everything under control and not to worry.

One day, a guy wanted to buy sneakers but we also became friends. I allowed him to get close to me because I had a crush on his sister. Not thinking, I started running my mouth, getting too excited, and telling him how easy it was to steal. That was a mistake. At the same time I called myself liking his sister, a state trooper was also interested in her. Her brother (my friend) told the state trooper what I told him about the clothing I'd stolen.

The next morning, I got a call from my probation officer, asking me to come to his office. He caught me off guard. I wasn't thinking about what we did. When I entered his office and shut the door, there was a guy with a long, brown trench coat standing by the door. He introduced himself as a detective. He asked me about breaking into the sneaker store and told me that he had pictures of me with the items on.

I said, "I didn't break into the sneaker store. I bought the stuff."

He asked, "From who?"

"I don't know the guy's name," I replied.

"I know that you're lying. I have statements from other people."

"I still don't know what you're talking about," I said. I stayed in the office for two hours before he finally allowed me to leave.

I rushed home, called everyone, and told them to move their stash to a different location because the police were on to us. I laid low for about a week, but to my surprise, they somehow rounded up the others.

One morning, there was a knock at the door. Two detectives greeted me and told me I was under arrest. They said they had signed statements from my friends, stating that I was the main culprit who stole all the stuff and gave it to them. I was arrested even though I didn't provide a signed statement.

I stayed in jail for almost two months. Renee came to see me and I could see the hurt and disappointment on her face. She had another month and a half before our baby would be born. I told her I was sorry and she continued to encourage me. She told me that she was there for me and that she was going to give my family the other part of the money to get me out.

I got out on a Thursday night, went home, ate a hot dinner, watched some television, and had a good night's sleep. I had to go see my parole officer the following day and I was placed under house arrest. I had to wear an ankle bracelet and be in the house at specific times.

It was my senior year and everyone knew what happened. I had to make up the two months I missed by staying after school every day.

• • •

Renee had a baby boy and it changed my entire life. I was so happy to be a father and to have a son. I was home all the time playing with him. I continued going to school, found a job, and stayed away from my codefendants. I didn't know who to trust. I was concerned about what the verdict from the court hearing was going to be. There was still no sentence and the devil was still trying to destroy me.

One summer afternoon, I came home from work and saw one of Renee's male friends in the house. He was trying to hug and kiss on her. He apologized but it was too late. The sight threw me into a rage and I lost it. My mind was unstable and I was angry and depressed. I was having mood swings, and thoughts of killing myself or someone else continued to plague my mind.

About seven months passed and I finally received a letter in the mail informing me of a new court date. When I went to court, the judge sentenced me to eighteen months in prison. My attorney pleaded with the court to reduce the sentence to six months because I had a newborn son but the judge denied the request because of my extensive record. Instead, he took back the eighteen months and gave me one year in the county jail. I started doing time immediately. Because I was still in school, I went in each Friday evening at six o'clock and got out each Sunday evening at six o'clock. This allowed me to finish my last year of high school. By the time I graduated, my parents had separated and didn't even come to my graduation.

After I graduated, I went back to jail full time to serve the remaining term on my sentence. I adapted very well to the jail life because many of my friends from the street were in there. To me, it was like boot camp.

Before I went back to jail, I had turned my life over to Christ because I wanted a new way of life for my son. I fasted every day from six o'clock in the morning until three o'clock in the afternoon. The inmates noticed that every time something provocative or sexual came on TV, I returned to my cell. The guys looked forward to watching soap operas just to see the women but I returned to my cell to read and pray. Several people told me there was a difference in me and asked me, "Why are you here?" The prison guards also noticed that I was different and they told me, "You don't belong here."

My relationship with God grew stronger. Even though I was in jail, I still felt free in my mind and in my spirit. My Uncle Lonnie stayed in touch with me by writing me letters and encouraging me to hang in there. The devil did not like that I was building up my relationship with God. He noticed the influence I had on the inmates and the guards.

On Thanksgiving Day, I woke up and asked the corrections officer if I could make a call so I could wish my son a happy Thanksgiving. My feelings for Renee were not as strong because while I was in jail I had time to reflect on things that took place when I was with her. I still had feelings for her but I was no longer in love with her.

When I called the house, a male voice greeted me on the other end of the phone. I asked for Renee and he said she was not there. Before I could ask who he was, he hung up. To me it sounded like it was her other son's father. I called back but no one answered. When I finally reached her by calling her mom's house, Renee told me that it was the maintenance man fixing something but I knew that was not the truth. As I matured in Christ, I realized it was the Holy Spirit telling me not to believe her.

I didn't know then that God would deal with me as a prophet. But just as clearly as I speak to another person standing in front of me is how clearly God was telling me it was the child's father, but I didn't need to worry because He was with me. Once I heard God's voice, my confidence in Him was built up.

I called my oldest sister to tell her what happened and I asked her to start bringing my son to the jail because I didn't want Renee to come there. I called Renee and told her that I no longer wanted to see her and she started crying. I felt no animosity or anger towards her. I just felt a sense of peace. I told her I wished her well and asked her to please take care of my son. Then I hung up the phone. After that, my sister brought my son to see me several times.

Since the devil saw that he couldn't get me to give up on God because of the phone call on Thanksgiving Day, he came up with something that took me nearly twenty years to accept.

On Christmas Eve, I prayed to God, asking Him to please allow me to be released from jail so I could be with my son. I pleaded with God, telling Him that it would be the first time to have Christmas with my son and that I would like to spend it with him. I continued to pray and fast that evening and into the morning.

On Christmas Day, at six o'clock in the morning, the corrections officer yelled, "Open up cell seven!" He told me that I had a visitor. He said it was my cousin, who was a pastor at my family's church. I jumped out of the bed thinking my prayers were answered but as I walked down the hall, again, the Holy Spirit spoke to me as clearly as if I was walking beside someone. "Brace yourself, he's come here to tell you that your son has passed away." My heart dropped, but there was still a sense of peace.

As I sat down at the table, my cousin asked, "How have you been?"

I said, "Okay. I know my son is gone."

"How do you know?"

I told him that something in my spirit had told me. He prayed with me and encouraged me but anger came over me.

I had written my cousin several letters asking him to visit me but the only time he came to visit was to tell me that my son had died. The previous month, he had come to the jail to visit another church member. All this was flashing through my mind while he talked to me. I couldn't believe that he came to see a church member but not his own cousin. He said I could call him if I needed him but I never did.

The Holy Spirit kept my mind in perfect peace just as God's Word states[3]. As I walked back to my cell, the guard told me to pack my stuff. I was going to be placed on twenty-four hour watch on F block. F block was known for the mentally insane inmates. They kept me there for about a month. I couldn't eat. I couldn't sleep. I lost weight. I cried and I prayed to keep my sanity. Several guards encouraged me to hang in there.

After a month, they moved me back to my regular block. When I went back to the block my personality shifted and I became a clown. I made people laugh so I didn't have to think. I stopped reading my Bible because I was angry with God. I believed I was cursed because when I fasted it brought back memories of my son's death.

About two weeks later, I received a letter about the possibility of entering the work release program. I wrote the judge a letter stating my case and in less than a month, I was out. On a one-year sentence, I had served six and a half months.

When I was released, my mind was confused and my heart was numb. I didn't go to the church. Instead, I hung out with my old crew. I started getting high, getting drunk, and sniffing cocaine to numb the pain of my loss. I also began shoplifting again.

Several people told me that there was something suspicious about my son's death. My neighbors told me that the father of Renee's other son was there that night. Renee's story was that she had to get up in the morning for work so she put my son in the bed with her eight-year-old son. When she got up in the morning, she claimed she found him lying stiff in the bed and didn't know whether her son rolled on top of him and didn't realize it or if our son had been turning in his sleep. The neighbors believed it was foul play because they saw her son's father leave early that morning. Then no more than thirty minutes later, the paramedics arrived. Renee never mentioned to the police that he had been there. She said she was there by herself.

To this day, I don't know if it was murder, foul play, or an accident. All I know is that my family told me that the coroner's report stated there was foul play. The police officer told my older sister that foul play meant that my son was murdered but the cause of death was undetermined, so they called it an accidental death. They suspected that Renee's son accidentally rolled on top of him and smothered him while he was asleep.

During this time, the devil convinced me that God was not real. My mind became more deviant, coming up with plans and schemes to survive. I was caught shoplifting again. It was a violation of my parole and I had to go back to jail and serve the remainder of my sentence. The other inmates told me that there were drugs and liquor in there and that people were smoking and drinking on Friday nights. To my surprise, it was happening on my block. They told me that different females came to visit their boyfriends and husbands, and brought the drugs up to the jail.

One Friday night, I went to the cell of one of the guys who worked in the kitchen with me and found out how it went down. We all met in a cell and had a joint. Everybody took a quick puff and then held the smoke in as long as possible because it was just one joint. They had me dip my cup in a garbage bag that was full of jail hooch. It was a homemade wine and the inmates would let it sit for about a week. After a week, they said it was ripe and ready. To my surprise, it got me high. It helped me to forget about all the drama and hell that I'd been through.

I didn't sense the devil riding my back anymore because I had joined him. I thought that every time I tried to fast, talk to or pray to God, something drastic would happen.

Chapter 6

NEW DOG, OLD TRICKS

While I was in jail, one of the guards introduced me to a pornography book. A spirit of sexuality was developing in me. The jail had become too crowded so they transferred me to another county jail. While I was there, I worked around female staff in the kitchen. They were probably twenty years older than me but one of them always made comments about how good I looked. I caught her staring at me when I walked past.

One day, she asked me to go to the cellar with her to unpack the delivery truck. While I unloaded the truck, she made comments about my strength. She was an older woman and not my type, but I had been in jail so long, anything would do as long as it was a female. She kissed me on the cheek several times. After a while, she told me about how her husband was not pleasing her. I told her that she wouldn't have to worry about me not being able to please her.

We decided that when the delivery truck came again, we would get intimate. When the day finally arrived, I went to the kitchen but she was not at work. To my surprise, when I was done working, one of the corrections officers told me to pack my bags. I was being transferred back to the other county jail and my release day was approaching.

As I became a mature Christian, I realized that every time I wanted to go all the way into something wrong, God was there interceding and fighting for me. I was a young black male and she was a young Caucasian woman. If something had taken place, she would have cried rape. I only had three weeks left to serve on my sentence. Had I been caught, I would have been penalized with more time than I could imagine.

I thank God for His Word. He will never leave us nor forsake us.[4] Even though I left Him, He stayed with me and fought for me. Sometimes, when we want things to happen, frustration, agony, and even rejection take over. We have to view it as God's protection. I know there are people who have gone through disappointments, devastation, rejection, and bad relationships, but hold your head up because often times this is God's way of protecting you from deeper hurt and regret.

. . .

My release date came and I finally got out, but the devil had created a male chauvinist and a gigolo. I went inside the jail weighing two hundred and thirty-five pounds. I came out weighing only one hundred and sixty-two pounds. Depression and working out had trimmed me up, but no one knew that the little boy in me was still hurting from abuse, and I was lonely. I went back to my parents' house and only stayed there for about a month. I was still feeling a sense of not being wanted in the house that I grew up in, so I moved back into Jerome's house. I had nowhere else to go and nowhere else to turn. I really didn't want to go back to his place because I knew it would take me back to a place where I knew I shouldn't go—drugs and alcohol. Old habits slowly returned but I continued working out and I had Jerome working out, too.

I was quiet and kept to myself, remembering much of the pain that I suffered when I was in jail. Often times I thought about my son's death, which caused me to start eating more. The word on the street was that Renee and her other son's father had married and moved down south. I wondered if my son's death was merely a part of their plan. Did they plan to kill my son and then move? I never ran into her on the street, but there were years of me plotting, of me wanting to see both of them hurt. Again, God intervened and never let that happen. I thank Him for that.

I didn't know at the time but now I know that my body was looking for an outlet to release the pain. I started sniffing cocaine and smoking weed again. I just couldn't get it together. The pain I had been through as a child and dealing with the shock and grief of my son's death was tearing me apart inside. I was back in shape and I was getting women but I was numb to life.

Jerome, his friend, Smitty, and me got together on weekends and sniffed cocaine. We would start around eleven o'clock in the morning and go until two o'clock the following morning. One day, we all went to Manhattan to buy a quarter of a kilo. It was about a three and a half hour drive from upstate New York to Manhattan. The plan was that we would get the package but we wouldn't sniff it until we got back. Everybody agreed.

After driving for a while, Smitty said he was getting tired. It was dark and we could barely see the road with all the snow blowing around us. We pulled over on the side of the highway and he opened up the package and took a couple hits of the coke. Before the rest of us could take a hit, we saw blue and red flashing lights coming up behind us. We panicked. It was a state trooper. We closed the package and Smitty put it under his leg. We didn't have time to stash it anywhere. The state trooper came up to Smitty's window.

"What's the problem here?"

"We pulled over because of the weather, to let the snow die down," Smitty said.

"Where are you coming from?" the officer asked.

"We're coming from the city. We were visiting our cousin," Smitty answered smoothly.

"Are you traveling with any guns or drugs in the car?" the trooper asked, shining his light into the car.

"You look like you're high. Step out of the car please."

My heart fell to my stomach.

Smitty stepped out of the car and as he did, he slipped the drugs under my leg. I was so nervous that I was shaking. I didn't want to go back in. I had just come home.

The trooper patted Smitty down and found half a bag of marijuana on him. He put him in handcuffs instantly and walked him to the back of the police car.

My mind was racing and I tried to stash the cocaine under the seat but another state trooper pulled up right next to us and shined his light in the car. My jacket was on the seat so I took the cocaine from under my leg and put it in the jacket.

The officer came around to my side of the car and ordered me to get out. I panicked. I was going to tell the truth—that the drugs weren't mine and that they belonged to Smitty. Instead, I kept my mouth shut, threw my jacket over my shoulders, put the cocaine under my armpit, and squeezed down on it. As the officer opened up the door, I asked him if he could back up because I couldn't get out the car. Again, God showed me that He was with me. The state trooper did something that I know he wasn't supposed to do. Instead of taking a few steps back while he watched me get out of the car, he turned his back towards me. By the time he turned back to me I had gotten out of the car, lifted my arm up, and let the cocaine drop in the snow. As he walked towards me, I covered up the cocaine with the snow.

He patted me down and told me to empty my pockets, but he didn't find anything. He took the flashlight and shined it on the ground where I was standing and then shined it inside the car. I'd never been so happy that we had a snow blizzard. The snow hit the ground and covered the package. I had buried the cocaine with my foot and the snow piled on top of it. The snow was still blowing so hard that he never even saw the cocaine. After they patted down Jerome and me, they told us to follow them to the nearest station because they were going to give our friend, Smitty, a ticket. Since he only had half bag of weed, it would be a misdemeanor, but he still had to go back to the station to be fingerprinted.

As we drove off, Jerome and I were thanking God at the same time. He asked me what I did with the cocaine. I told him I buried it in the snow at mile marker one sixty-two. At the station, they fingerprinted Smitty, gave him a ticket, and let him go. When we got in the car Smitty immediately asked what I did with the cocaine. I told him he was wrong for sliding the drugs under my leg. He knew that if I had been caught, I would have taken the rap and went back to jail. He didn't apologize. He had no remorse for what he did. He asked if I remembered where I buried it. I lied and told him I buried it at mile marker one forty-two.

When we returned to the post, Smitty jumped out of the car and shoveled the snow with his bare hands until he reached the ground. He repeatedly asked me if I was sure it was the right place. I told him I was sure. We were out there for over an hour. Eventually, he got back in the car and started crying. Through his tears, he told us that he used his girlfriend's rent money and the kids' Christmas money to buy the drugs and he didn't know what he was going to tell her. I didn't flinch or budge. I didn't care about his tears. All I thought was that he tried to set me up. We made it back home safely and dropped him off.

Jerome and I went home and got some sleep. When we woke up that evening we drove back to mile post one sixty-two. We shoveled out the snow and the package was right there. We put the cocaine in the car but this time we had a jug of water. If we were pulled over again, we would put the cocaine in the jug of water so it could dissolve and then pour the water on the car mats. We didn't worry about the mats being white with residue because when it snowed and we got back into the car, the snow and the salt from the roads would make the mats white, too. It was the perfect plan, but luckily, we never had to use it.

We made it back home, called a couple of friends, and partied. We sniffed a lot and then bagged up some to sell. When we unraveled the kilo, there were ten bundles of wax paper wrapped up and attached to the cocaine. We didn't know what it was but we took it to another friend and he told us it was heroin. We didn't know anything about heroin, so we gave it to one of our friends to sell.

There were about eight or nine of us but there was plenty of cocaine for everyone to party. I watched people do things with cocaine that I'd never seen before. One guy took the cocaine and sprinkled it in his eyes. We sniffed some, we cooked some into crack, and then we bought weed and smoked the crack cocaine in a blunt with the weed. We sniffed and smoked for about three weeks straight. We had so much cocaine in our bodies that we couldn't sleep. We had to smoke a ton of weed and drink a lot of alcohol just to bring us down. We didn't eat either. The cocaine wouldn't let us do it.

There were times when my heart was racing from all the drugs, but when you're an addict you don't even care if you overdose, you're just chasing the high. When we went out we took some of the cocaine with us to trick. We picked up women who liked to get high. One night we picked up a woman who was much older than us. She was probably in her early thirties. She was a prostitute who exchanged sex for drugs. There were four of us that night and we took her home with us. Our plan was to get her high and run a train on her. We would all takes turns having sex with her. That night we sniffed so much cocaine that when it was time for us to perform we couldn't. This went on for about an hour. Nobody could get stimulated at all.

Another hour went by and the cocaine and alcohol were beginning to wear off. She wanted more but we didn't have any more to give her, so she got dressed and ran down the stairs, telling us that we were going to pay. She yelled, "Rape!"

I turned to Jerome, Jerome turned to Dewayne, and we said, "Do you hear that?" She was knocking on doors and screaming. We had to move quickly. We changed the sheets and in seconds, we had changed the living room around. We changed the bedroom around, too, just in case she brought the police back and described the way the house looked. We snatched clothes, ran out the back door, drove off in the car, and we went to stay at Jerome's cousin's house.

Jerome's dad was an ex-cop and he called one of the detectives. They verified that she made a call that night to say three guys raped her but she didn't know our names. Jerome's dad told the detective the story. The detective confirmed that she had a large amount of cocaine in her system and they had taken her to the hospital. The hospital determined there were no signs of rape— no forced entry, no scratches, and no bruises.

We hid out for two weeks until Jerome's father came to where we were hiding out and said the detective called to say that the woman dropped the charges. Again, I thanked God because I knew He was watching over me. I already had a record and to be convicted of rape would have gotten me seven years or more back in jail.

We decided to chill out for a while. I found a part-time job, started working, stayed off the street, stayed away from the club, and went to church. It was difficult for me to be in church because half the church knew that I had been incarcerated and I could sense that some were judging me and talking about me. Some members acted like they were nervous whenever I sat near them.

One thing that I just couldn't stop doing was getting high. There were times we would go to church and sit on the back pew, still high and drunk. I noticed that people would talk to all my friends but they wouldn't say much to me because I was known as the criminal.

Eventually, I stopped going to church and started going back to the club.

Chapter 7

IT'S GETTING CRAZY

I still felt worthless. Every time I thought that everything would be okay, something set me back. I thought the people in the church would be more understanding but they weren't. This brought on fear, insecurities, and the spirit of rejection. Women threw themselves at me but I was still depressed and lonely. I walked around the club with women pulling on me and calling my name but I kept walking. When I saw someone I was interested in, I approached her and talked to her. I didn't have a problem talking to women. Even when I was overweight, there were more women. I often thought, *what do they want with a guy like me?*

There were times in my life when I continued to indulge in overeating. My addiction to food started when I was a kid. Every time there was a tragedy, I found something to eat. My weight went up and down. People picked on me and called me names but they had no idea that I had given my own names to the extra weight. Twenty extra pounds was called rejection. Another twenty pounds was called pain. Another ten pounds was called depression.

There were times in my life when I'd gotten so big that I couldn't fit into my clothes. I would sit and meditate on everything that went wrong in my life and just eat. Women would say, "Look at the cute, handsome bear." They didn't know that I couldn't stand living in my own body. I developed a cycle. When I got bigger, I was forced to either buy more clothes or work out. I chose to work out, and when I worked out I became a fanatic.

Even when I was in shape, I still had insecurities. It brought more women into my life but instead of me receiving their compliments, I chose to be conceited and to get back at the world. I dated women and quickly realized that for them, it wasn't about relationships, it was just about sex. That never worked out for me. I was looking for a family. I dated women who had kids because I was good with kids. My friends used to tell me, "You can't take a whore out of the club and make her a housewife." Nevertheless, I tried.

I had a strong personality and all my women knew that I belonged to a gang. My mental state had shifted into killer mode. If I went to a club and ran into a woman I was dating and saw her dancing with or talking to another guy, my mind flipped. Anger rose up in me. The guys knew the gang I was in, so when they saw me they walked away. The women in my life were fond of me being a thug and a protector. They would stop going out and get themselves together. They went back to school, got jobs, and raised their kids the way they were supposed to be raised. I didn't know I had a gift from God—the gift of influence.

One day in the club, I ran into a woman I had adored since high school. Sasha was one of the most popular girls in the school. She had a nice ride and she was every man's dream from head to toe. She was in college and when she saw me after I was released from jail, her mind was blown. We hit it off right away. Every time I went to the club, I hoped she would be there. We talked, got to know each other, and started dating. We would leave the club and go to her mom's house to hang out and talk all night, but there were two problems—her mom and her friend, Tammy.

Even though Sasha was in her twenties, her mom was very controlling. I threw rocks at her window so she could sneak out and we could go stay at my place, even though I was still staying with Jerome. Other times, I would be out with my friends and when I came home she would be there waiting for me. All of my friends were cool with her. We all knew her from growing up with us.

Another problem was that both of us had quick tempers. Sasha had a smart mouth and could get me going by saying the smallest thing. We were like oil and water sometimes. I loved her but as soon as she started yelling at me, I had flashbacks of my Mom and I would just lose it. Sometimes our fights got physical.

One night, she went to the club looking for me. When she realized I wasn't there, she came to Jerome's house and banged on the door. It was two o'clock in the morning. When a woman is scorned, she gains power. She banged on the door until one of Jerome's family members finally let her in the house.

At the time, I had another woman in the house with me. Sasha banged on the bedroom door, shouting at me to let her in. At first, I acted like I was sleeping, but she began kicking on the door louder and louder. Twenty minutes later, she literally kicked down the door. The girl in the room with me was terrified. Sasha ran towards her but I held her back and the girl ran out of the room, out of the house, and all the way home.

I told Sasha that I was sleeping and that my brother had the girl there. She calmed down and we talked for a while before she finally went home. As soon as she left, I called my brother and told him to cover for me. Like clockwork, she called him the next morning, and he did as I asked. Because we were all friends, Jerome laughed it off and fixed the door. He said she was just being crazy, but we all looked at each other and said, "Whew! That was a close one."

The next time she came over and couldn't get in, I wasn't doing anything. Sasha said that someone told her they saw me out in the club with another woman. I told her that they didn't know what they were talking about. Even my roommate said that we never left the house. I was using my hands to explain when she pulled a grilling fork out of her purse. Before I could stop her, there was blood gushing from my hand where she had driven the fork through it. Jerome lunged at her and took the fork while I wrapped my hand with a towel.

I was so mad that I started yelling at the top of my lungs. We had a blowout argument and made so much noise that the family downstairs called the police. I was still angry when the police asked if I wanted to press charges, but after I cooled off I told the officer I just didn't want her over there anymore. They escorted her out of the house and I thanked God that nothing else happened that day.

I finally found out that her mother had told her the lies. When I confronted her mom, she confessed and said that she was just joking and she didn't think Sasha was going to take her seriously. Her mother felt guilty so she brought me pain pills and was nice to me for a while. She even told me that if I wanted to come to her house to visit her daughter, I could.

Once Sasha found out that her mom had lied, she was sorry. Her mom was always in our business because she was overprotective of her daughter. The more trouble she started, the closer Sasha came to me, and before we knew it, she was pregnant.

Shortly after we found out Sasha was pregnant, her friend, Tammy, began starting trouble in our relationship. I used to date Tammy and when she saw Sasha and me, she said things to upset her. Sasha was attractive but she could fight. She wasn't that tall, but she could hold her own. All the girls knew that, including Tammy. She just couldn't stand the fact that I had moved on and was dating Sasha.

One day, Tammy and I were talking outside of the club and Sasha showed up. She was pregnant and she got out of the car smiling. She walked up to us and smacked Tammy down to the ground. She had a way of not letting you know she was angry. She would approach you with a smile and then out of nowhere she would attack you.

Meanwhile, my cocaine habit got worse. I started picking up other women and getting high with them in hotels. Afterwards, I would come home at five or six o'clock in the morning. Sometimes I came home and Sasha wouldn't be there but she left notes telling me that she was at her mom's house.

One day while we were at home having some family time, Sasha came out the bedroom and water was pouring down her leg. She said her water broke, but I didn't know what that meant. Her mom rushed over and took her to the hospital while I stayed home with Sasha's daughter, who was still asleep.

To this day, I regret not letting go of the anger I had towards her mom. I wasn't willing to get in the car with her to take Sasha to the hospital. During Sasha's entire pregnancy, her mom and I argued. She told Sasha that she was carrying a little demon in her belly. The truth is that she never forgave me for taking Sasha out of her house at the age of twenty-four. She was using Sasha, taking her money, and manipulating her. When Sasha wouldn't give in, she called her and cussed her out, calling her all kinds of names. It made me so angry that it felt like a fire was inside of me.

Sasha had a daughter by another man and Sasha's mom tried to make things bad between Sasha and me by spoiling Sasha's daughter. She would say things like, "I don't want your unborn baby around my granddaughter." Her mom was known as the voodoo woman and people believed it. However, because of the relationship I had with God, she didn't bother me. She would say stuff to me but I would tell her that God wouldn't allow it and she would walk away.

I was so happy to have another boy because my first son had passed away. However, I had one problem that I wanted to kick—drugs and alcohol. I continued getting high and drinking, even after my son, Daeon, was born. I would be out all night and then I would come home and make promises to Sasha that I would stop hanging out so much.

There were times I would kick the habit and go at least twenty to thirty days clean, but then I would start hanging around my boys, and the more we hung out, the more drugs we used. We bought crack, mixed it with weed, put it in a blunt, and smoked it. It was a mellow high because it was an upper and a downer going at the same time. This became so addicting to me that when I got my income tax refund, I blew it all in one night on getting high.

I got high so much that I began accusing Sasha of seeing someone else. She always talked about a coworker that was very nice to her, but she said I didn't have to worry because he was gay. Well, one day I was getting high with my friends and I found his phone number in her car. I flipped out. I went upstairs and pushed her against the wall.

After Daeon was born, Sasha's mother came to visit her grand-daughter but not her grandson. On birthdays, she bought presents for her granddaughter but not for Daeon. She was angry when I made sure he had presents for his birthday, whether I bought them or stole them. I was overprotective with Daeon, due to my first son passing away. I watched the way people held him, often threatening people that they had better not drop him. I had a fear of him dying.

When Daeon was older, I got a steady job in construction and brought home a decent paycheck each week after taxes. Along with my regular hours, there was overtime. I didn't mind work-ing the overtime because I knew it was money for getting high. I thought I had it made. I was in my early twenties and making more money than people twice my age, but my relationship with Sasha was ending because of her family problems.

When her brother came home from college, he and Sasha's mom came to our house. We shook hands and I said, "What's up man?" As I led them upstairs, her mom whispered something in his ear and he came running after me. Sasha's mom told him I'd been giving his sister black eyes. It wasn't true and it was the final straw.

I couldn't let her mom run our relationship. Maybe Mr. Softy could do it, but I'm not that guy. The problem was that my heart had changed and I didn't want to kick down doors anymore. God changed my heart. When Sasha left to visit her sister in Califor-nia, I moved out and never lived with her again. The only time I wanted to see her was when I was coming to get my son.

I went into a deep depression. I cleaned up my act and stopped getting high. I felt like a whole new world was getting ready to open up to me.

Chapter 8

NEW LOVE

I was the only black person on the construction site and every day I went to work, people had black jokes. One time they invited me to a restaurant to eat. When we went into the restaurant, they made a joke and asked if the 'black boy' should eat in the back or in the front. I was mad. I reported the jokes to upper management, but they laughed it off and said that my coworkers were just joking. I felt like the odd man out.

One day I asked my coworkers for a mask because the paint fumes were making me dizzy. They told me to go back to work and to stop complaining. I fainted, tumbled off the bridge, landed in the creek, and passed out. I couldn't swim. Thank God, someone came down there and pulled me out of the creek. My supervisor brushed it off and told me to go back to work. Everyone looked at him like he was crazy. I was in a daze and my back and legs were hurting. Finally, they called an ambulance that took me to the hospital.

At the hospital, the doctors examined me but couldn't find anything. While I was getting dressed, one of the nurses asked another nurse, "Do you know who he is? That's Joe Blackshear's nephew." My uncle Joe was heavily involved in politics and had worked on campaigns for the mayor. Fortunately, another doctor knew my uncle, so he took me back and did a much more thorough exam. He found that when I moved my chin to my chest, it caused severe pain down my back. The doctor immediately wrote a prescription and told me to stay out of work for at least three weeks. He also said that I should receive one hundred percent disability pay while I was out.

Suddenly, the owner of the company was calling me and being very nice to me. He asked if my time off from work was because of the black jokes he didn't address. He told me that I didn't have to worry anymore because he'd told the other employees to leave me alone. He also said that if I wanted to return to work, I could come back the next day. What he didn't know was that the doctor had told me to get an attorney. When I told the owner that I couldn't speak to him because I had an attorney, he cussed at me. I told my attorney and gave him the owner's phone number. I never heard from the guy again.

While I was on disability, I was paid as if I was still working. I was making one hundred percent full pay just sitting at home. After a month went by, the company sent me to their doctor to be reevaluated and to determine what percentage of pay I should receive. Their doctor said eighty percent, but my doctor still said one hundred percent. While we continued going back and forth to court, I stayed at one hundred percent pay. This continued for about three months but soon sadness and depression kicked in. My doctor told my attorney and me to be careful because they would be following me. I was paranoid, but again, God looked out for me.

It just so happened that I had moved next door to my kindergarten teacher. I found out one day when she rang my doorbell and told me, "Mr. Blackshear, you don't remember me, but I was your kindergarten teacher. A man came to visit me and said he would pay me good money if I allowed him to sit and watch you for about three or four hours." It surprised me that my employer would go that far to try to find fault in my claim. After our conversation, I was very cautious whenever I left the house. The doctor gave me a neck brace and a cane to relieve some of the pressure from my back. To this day, I know God was with me.

• • •

One evening, I was out with my cousin when I saw a woman walking. I stopped my truck in the middle of the street, got out, approached her, and asked, "What can I do for you?" We talked and had already walked halfway down the block when she asked me, "What are you going to do with your truck?" I told her not to worry about it. My cousin was in the truck and I knew he would move it for me.

We kept walking and talking, and before I knew it, I had walked her home, which was about seven blocks from where we'd met. Her name was Cheryl. I tried to impress her by pulling out a wad of money and telling her I was going to pick her up the next day to take her shopping and to lunch. She smiled, gave me her number, and said to call her. I went back to my truck and my cousin said, "Oh my God. How did you pull that?"

I had never seen a woman like Cheryl before. She had a very different look, a different style, and I'd never seen her in the neighborhood. She lived in Queens, but she was born in Nicaragua. I was mesmerized. We clicked right away and within two weeks, we had built a relationship.

When Sasha returned to New York, everyone told her I was riding around with a beautiful young woman in my truck. I had called Sasha while she was still in California and told her that I was seeing someone else and I didn't want her to come back and start trouble. I told her to leave Cheryl alone.

Chapter 9

DRIVER

I continued developing a relationship with Cheryl. She had a young daughter and all three of us moved into a big seven-bedroom house. I felt like my life was getting ready to take off in a good direction. We instantly became a family. We started going to church together, eating dinner together, taking long drives, and going to parks. We did everything I wanted to do when I lived at home with my family. There was just one problem—Cheryl had dated a drug dealer who was murdered less than a year earlier. Sometimes she had complete emotional breakdowns. Even though I should have been compassionate, having gone through so much in my own life, I was upset that she still had memories of someone else.

I could have been more supportive of Cheryl but what could I do? I wasn't healed from my own pains, hurts, and setbacks in life. I was selfish and I wanted her to understand more about my pain than me understanding hers. This caused problems in our relationship. I realized that I moved too fast by moving her into a house without allowing her to heal from the pain of her past.

The one thing that was impressive about Cheryl was her loyalty. She was still attached to some of her girlfriends that were dating friends of her late boyfriend. I was a little insecure when they came by the house to visit and talked to her about him. I told her that I didn't want her friends to come to my house if they couldn't respect me and not talk about her former boyfriend in my presence and in my home.

We were dating for about four months when she found out she was pregnant. I was excited but she wasn't. She didn't feel that she would be able to bring a child into the world while she was still so emotionally torn apart over the murder of her late boyfriend. She made a decision to get rid of the baby. This upset me and I felt betrayed. I stayed with her but all I could think about was revenge and that meant seeking other women. I was drifting away—slowly, but surely.

As I continued to search for significance, I realized that I didn't have an identity. I tried to connect to everything and to everyone to find acceptance. Even though I couldn't see it at the time, Cheryl accepted the God in me, but I let the devil fool me into believing that in order for her to accept me, I had to become a drug dealer.

When I get into something, I try to become the best at it, so when it was time for me to start selling drugs, I joined one of the biggest, established organizations in New York. My life changed drastically. I no longer saw the people who grew up with me and we would never interact again. Everything became about cars, traveling, homes, and money. I also learned that if I was going to sell drugs, I had better be strapped. I didn't know much about guns but I learned enough to be a part of an organization that was running them.

The head of the organization invited me to become his driver. I was excited and I gained respect from people in the street because when they saw him, they saw me. For a while, this brought popularity but it also brought attention to me from the police. When I wasn't driving him around, I was on the block waiting for the soldiers to finish selling off their packages. My responsibility was to collect their money and to give them new packages to sell. I made crazy money.

I played dice with guys who had five thousand to ten thousand dollars in their pockets at all times. One night, I was down to my last five dollars, after coming there with about three hundred. It was my turn to roll the dice and after several hours, my five bucks grew to seven thousand. One thing you need to know about playing dice and winning is that when you take other people's money, they want you to give them a fair chance to get their money back.

I left the game and went to the bathroom. While I was in there, I called my crew and asked them to come back because I didn't feel comfortable. I stuffed the money into my socks and into each pocket while I talked to them. I told them to bring their guns, even though I knew their guns would be checked at the door. That was my purpose for telling them to bring them. I wanted people to see that we were strapped.

When they came to the door, I rolled the dice and told the guys at the table I was only going to do a couple more rolls, and then I was gone. One guy was upset and felt I should stay there all night so he could try to win his money back.

One of my crew said, "If he's ready to leave, we're leaving." Everyone respected that and it was a wrap. As I left the place, I counted the money—it was seventy-three hundred dollars.

I was making crazy money but that didn't change how I felt inside and it didn't help my relationship. When I went home, I was still miserable because we were living separate lives. I thought that we were living the life Cheryl wanted but I could clearly see that was not true. She never turned back to the drug game. She remained on the other side and became everything God wanted her to become.

When I met Cheryl, she didn't have a high school diploma. I was amazed as I watched her get her GED and continue on to college. She also got closer to God. I was upset because I was the one who brought her to the church but I found myself slipping away from the church. I was the one who had a strong relationship with God but I was allowing the devil to pull me back into a world of darkness—the world of drugs, alcohol, partying, and the new world of dealing drugs.

Cheryl changed right before my eyes. Everywhere I went with her, men and women commented on how beautiful she was. My anger, frustration, and jealously crept in and I thought she was trying to be better than me, so when people gave her compliments, it upset me. The devil had me. The street life had taken control of me and I enjoyed it. The devil knew that everything he put in front of me would get me to walk away from God.

For some reason, even though I stopped going to church, I never stopped praying. I prayed and talked to God when I was selling drugs, driving my boss around in the car, and even when I was playing dice. It was a habit. I believe that constant prayer is what protected me from dying and receiving jail time while I was out there in the world.

One Sunday, I was coming from church and I told my friend to drop me off on the block where they were selling drugs and playing dice. One of the guys said, "Bless (my street name), how in the world can you go to church and you sell more dope and run more guns than the majority of us out here?"

My answer was simple. "Even though I'm selling drugs and guns, I can at least give God one day of my time and step away from this."

As he rolled the dice he said, "Wow. I never thought of anything like that. Doesn't God hate people like us?"

"No."

"How do you know that, Bless?"

"I just know."

I knew God cared about me. I didn't know how much He loved me, but I knew He cared about me. I remembered going to church with my uncle when I was living at home with my parents, and the things my uncle told me stayed in my spirit. God already knew that I would walk away from the church, but I couldn't walk away from His Holy Spirit, which was imparted in me.

• • •

Although Cheryl and I continued dating, we grew further apart. There were times I came home from the streets at four or five in the morning. She was asleep but there would be a trail of notes left in the house. One of the notes was on the door and said, "Waited up . . . got tired . . . your food is in the oven." As I took my food out of the oven, there was another note, "I hope you like it. If not, wake me up and I'll see what else I can fix." Every note ended the same way, "P.S. If you want me to get up with you just wake me up." The devil had me so blind that I couldn't see that this was the very thing I wanted her to do. I desperately wanted to serve God so we could become a family.

I had one friend that I stayed in touch with who never sold drugs. Andre was a person that I could talk to and he gave me guidance about life. I appreciate his friendship to this day. He always had a plan (and a few scams) but he was always trying to do better. I kept him as a friend because I loved hanging around with people who were going somewhere.

He came to my house one night and I began the routine of taking my food out of the oven, but this time I had to use the bathroom. While I was gone, he read Cheryl's note and said, "Bless, you are stupid. Not only do you have one of the finest girls in New York, but you also got a girl who's willing to look out for you, even when you're in the street. She doesn't go to clubs, drink, or smoke. Man, you need to wake up before it's too late."

By the time Andre told me this, I was already deep into the bondage of the street world. At the same time, I wanted to give up the street life to make my relationship with Cheryl work, but fear and a lack of trust had become roadblocks. I continued hanging out in the streets and my drug selling increased. I also slipped further away from God.

One weekend, Cheryl went back to Queens to visit a friend. While she was gone I continued partying and another woman came into my life. I was previously involved with this woman but we broke it off because she became pregnant by another guy. Being with her was easy. She was already caught up in that street life. As I look back, I see how the devil blinded me and made me think that something of God was bad, while something of the devil was good.

I called Cheryl one day while she was still visiting in Queens and a guy answered the phone and said, "Who is this?" Her friend snatched the phone, apologized, and said that her boyfriend had answered the phone, but something in my spirit told me that she was lying. Cheryl told me that she was going to be down there for a couple more days. My antennae went up when I heard the guy in the background asking her how long she was going to be on the phone. I was angry and I thought about going to Queens but the street life had me caught up. When I hung up, my heart dropped because I realized that I was still in love with her.

I called her later but I couldn't reach her. Finally, she called me back after several hours and told me that she would be home early in the morning on the bus. As I sat and prayed, I told God that I was going to come clean and tell her everything.

When I picked her up from the station, we both sat quietly in the car. She asked how things went while she was gone and I told her they were fine. I told her I had to confess to her and she said the same thing to me. We went out for lunch and I let her talk first. She told me about a guy she met in Queens. She told me that they didn't do anything sexually but she did kiss him. My heart dropped. She asked me what I had to tell her but I couldn't even speak. I got up, left money for lunch, gave her cab fare, and left.

I went back home, packed my bags, and went to stay at my friend's house. I couldn't sleep that whole night because Cheryl was banging on the door with a bat and shouting that she knew someone was up there with me. It wasn't true. Finally, I opened the door and she asked if I would come back to the house so we could talk. I went with her but I was angry and upset. I told her that as long as I was there, no one would sit on my furniture, and then I threw the furniture over the porch. It wasn't about the furniture. It was about finding a way to hurt her.

Our relationship was over and that led me to drink more, get high more, and just hang out. I had money, but I was depressed because I had lost my honey. I didn't see her for weeks because I stayed away. While I was on the block one day, one of my friends told me that he'd seen Cheryl with a guy walking through the park. I acted like I didn't care but it bothered me.

Eventually, I began dating a woman from Colombia. When people saw me with her, they told me that she looked two times better than Cheryl. I didn't pay attention to how the other girl looked. I was just using her to get back at Cheryl. She was just another woman who was willing to do whatever I asked.

One day my sister had a gathering at her house. She said she didn't mind if I came but warned me not to start any trouble. I brought my new girlfriend and her friends to the party. Cheryl was there and I could see from the look on her face that she was upset. Everything worked according to the plan. Cheryl and her friend left. I knew I'd made her upset, but I didn't want her to leave the party.

Months went by and I hadn't seen her. On a cold afternoon while I was standing on the block, I saw a guy approaching me. He asked if I knew who was selling weed. He was wearing a hat that looked familiar. I had given that hat to Cheryl. I found out that he was the same guy who answered the phone when she went to visit her friend in Queens, but I let him go.

Four months later, Cheryl came to me and said that she was leaving New York to be with someone who had enlisted in the military. I pleaded with her and begged her not to leave. I told her I wanted to try to work things out. She cried and said I was a very different person. A week later, she was gone. I sold the house. I didn't want to go back in there with old memories.

Chapter 10

WHAT'S BEEF?

Every day it seemed like I was selling drugs from sunrise to sunset. I shifted from hanging with local hustlers to hustlers who were killers. I just didn't care. I started going hard in the street. At dice games when I got upset I told them that they'd better be careful or they may not live to see the next day. Because of the crew I was in, it put fear into people who knew me.

My crew was hard but we were warned about a crew from East New York because they were grimy. Nevertheless, I let the devil ride my back and I continued hanging in the streets to try to ease my pain. I knew that the devil had me becoming something that God didn't want me to become, and one day I found out why.

A guy named Ron, one of the crew members from East New York, started running his mouth when we were playing dice. I wasn't thinking and I let anger take over. I told him he'd better watch his mouth before he found himself buried in the snow. Now I was in an organization I'd never been in and I didn't know all the rules and regulations yet. Ron's right hand man was right beside him, but I didn't know. Later, I found out that they were asking people about me. I hadn't hurt anyone or shot anybody. The only thing people knew about me is that I ran the streets with my crew and I was a driver. I had not established a name yet, so people said, "Oh, that's just Bless."

One night, me and a guy from my crew were on our way to a concert when I ran into Mike. He was a friend of Ron, the guy who I'd threatened to bury in the snow. I told him I was getting ready to go to a concert and he asked me if we could give him a ride. He was in the passenger seat and I was in the back seat. In the game, you don't trust anybody, so you don't want anybody sitting behind you. You always want to keep your eyes on the other guy. Street life is real grimy that way. As he gave directions to where he wanted to be dropped off something in my spirit didn't feel right. When he called my name, he reached into his pants, and I jumped out of the car and ran. Remember the story in the Bible about Lot's wife looking back?[5] Well, I did the same thing—I looked back and I saw them laughing. I stopped running, turned around, and asked them why they were laughing.

"Why did you run, man?" Mike said.

"Why were you calling my name and digging in your pants?"

"Man, I can't believe you thought I was trying to rob you. Yo, Bless, that's foul. Why you gonna accuse me of something like that?" Mike said.

"Don't worry about that. Just forget it," I said.

As I went to get into the car, he backed up into a dark spot and told me to come over there. I said, "Nah, everything's good. I'm not coming over there."

Suddenly, he pulled out a gun. I ran and he chased me. The next thing I knew, I was on the ground with him standing right on top of me. Someone said, "Don't shoot! Someone's on the porch!" I lifted my head and saw a man standing on the porch of a clean white house and he was smoking a cigarette.

Mike was known for shooting people in the head at point-blank range, but he didn't shoot me. He robbed me and then ran away. Eventually, I got up and started walking toward the guy on the porch, but when I got to the house, it was old and abandoned and there was no one there. The old guy who had been smoking the cigarette wasn't there and there were no ashes on the ground.

I write this now to say that no one can tell me God isn't real.

Later, I called my crew and told them what happened. Since I hung out with the leader, he instantly said that we had to retaliate.

Another member of the crew asked if I wanted to retaliate that night. I told him that I needed time to think. It wasn't his beef so I couldn't accept his offer.

When I woke up the next day, I was still angry. It was summer time and it had to be at least ninety-five degrees outside. I went out on the block wearing a long leather coat. I had a nine-millimeter gun in my pocket and a sawed off shotgun in my coat. I stayed on the block for over an hour but no one would come near me. Everyone kept asking me if we were good. That was the code on the block to make sure I wasn't looking for them. Everyone knew that if I was on the block with a long length leather coat on, I was strapped. I told everyone that I was looking for Mike but nobody had seen him.

Hours passed and I didn't see him come out on the block so I went home. My clothes were soaking wet from sweat. I was angry that my plan failed but as I look back, I see that God was protecting me. God knew that if I saw him I was going to shoot him and He intervened. Nevertheless, that didn't stop me.

Later that night, I went to a concert—it was a two-day event. I wore my forty below boots with a pair of jeans, a sweatshirt, and a hat. I had a twenty-five and a nine-millimeter stuffed in the bottom of my boot. If I saw Mike, I was going to blast him.

When I pulled up to the concert, there were cops outside with a metal detector and a wand. My heart raced but I walked through anyway. To my amazement, I walked right through and the metal detector didn't pick up anything.

When I got into the concert, I looked around to see if Mike was there but I didn't see him anywhere. Then unexpectedly, someone touched me on my back and said, "Yo, Bless. Sorry about robbing you. See me tomorrow on the block and I'm going to give you your money back." It was Mike! Fury and fear entered me at the same time. I bent down, unlaced my boots, and took out the gun. By the time I stood up someone had yelled, "Gun!" Over three thousand people started running toward me and I fell on my back.

I was being trampled. I couldn't move and I couldn't breathe but I managed to get on my stomach. That gave me enough strength to maneuver my body and push off with my arms. The only gun I saw was the twenty-five.

I ran through the crowd telling people to get out of my way. I wound up in the women's bathroom. They were on one side of the stalls yelling and screaming and I was on the other side.

I yelled, "Everybody shut up and calm down!"

Out of the crowd my Jamaican girl said, "Bless!"

"Yo, what's up? I'm about to get up out of this bathroom. I'm not going to get trapped in here," I replied.

All the women said, "Take us with you!"

"Follow me," I said.

My hand was on the gun in my pocket with the safety off. If I saw Mike, I was going to blast him on the spot. When I made it to the car, I couldn't find my crew so my friend's girlfriend gave me a ride home. As we talked in the car, I shared my problem with her. She told me that her boyfriend, Nelson, got into a fight and he pulled out HIS gun. Before he could pull the trigger, someone yelled, "Gun!"

I tell you, God is amazing, because if I had my gun out, I would have shot Mike in the back. God allowed Nelson and me to pull out our guns at the same time for people to yell and cause a distraction. I went home that night and decided to lay low. I continued hanging out and partying but I did it on the opposite side of town until the coast was clear and my name was no longer ringing in the streets.

One night, when I was coming from a party, I saw Mike walking. I had my gun on me so I pulled my car two blocks in front of him, turned off the lights, got out of the car, and ran between the houses in the direction he would be walking. I waited for what should have been only five minutes before he walked past me but it turned into twenty minutes. I came out from between the houses and looked down the street but I didn't see anyone. I got back in my car and circled the blocks but he was nowhere in sight.

Chapter 11

GOD BLOCKED IT

I always kept my relationship with God. At the same time I was thinking about harming someone, I was still thinking about God. I went home wondering why I couldn't get Mike. Anger festered in me because he robbed me. All I could think about was revenge.

One night, I went to the store about two in the morning to buy some blunts. When I turned around, he was behind me. My whole body trembled. I didn't have a gun and my boys weren't with me. I said in a crackling voice, "What's up, Mike?" I could barely talk. We stared at each other until I started walking out of the store, but I went back in to get something else. I just knew that when I left his boys would be outside waiting for me. I at least wanted to leave the store before him. I headed for the front door praying to God at the same time.

Instantly, it came to my spirit to open the door so the camera could catch me leaving the store. I held the door wide open so the camera could see me. I was hoping the camera would catch me leaving and at the same time capture enough of the parking lot so that if I walked outside and someone started shooting, the camera would catch it. I didn't want to let go of the door. The shorty in my car was looking at me in amazement.

I could hear myself walking towards the car. My heart was thundering, my hands were shaking, and my knees were knocking. In my mind, I heard gunshots. It's funny how your mind can take over with false evidence appearing real (FEAR). I finally made it to the car, shaking and in disbelief. To my surprise, the only car outside was my car. There was nobody else out there.

When I got home, I loaded my gun, placed my chair in front of the door, paced the floor, and waited for someone to come in. I passed out at about three in the morning. When I woke up, it was after nine. I jumped up and checked my body. When I realized I wasn't hurt, my mind went blank, and I thought to myself, *what do I need to do?* It was time to take the beef to another level.

I was in the store that afternoon when a young soldier came to me and said, "Hey, do you know Mike? He put out a contract on you. He said he would pay somebody to take you off the street." When I heard this, I thought, *what have I gotten myself into?* I thought about my son, my mother, and my family. In the drug game, if they can't get you, they come after your family. I laid low and rode by their houses to make sure everything was okay.

I called my Mom and Sasha every now and then to make sure they were okay. I told Sasha to be careful, but to my surprise, she had already heard about what was going on. This time I was grateful that when she and I separated she started dating that guy from East New York. Her new boyfriend had already told Mike and his crew not to bring that mess where he laid his head. Since he put that word out and Sasha was staying with him, I knew my son was protected.

When the leader of my crew found out what was going on, he was disgusted. He came to my sister's house and told me he had hired a hit man from New York City. He was coming the next day to take care of it. He asked me how I wanted it to happen. I told him to let me think about it. He told me that he needed an answer by noon the next day.

I thought about my Mom and my son. I didn't want to start a war because I knew that they knew where my Mom and son stayed. I prayed and talked to God. My heart was shifting and I really felt like getting revenge. I met the hit man at noon the next day. He told me how it would happen and about his plan to scope out Mike's daily pattern for a week. That gave me more time to think.

I started hanging out with the hit man, showing him different spots where Mike's crew hung out. We rode around and talked. I tried to get into his head by asking him questions. As we talked, I found out he had a major drug problem. I shared with him how I had smoked crack cocaine mixed with weed but because I was making money in the organization, my dope habit had stopped for about two years. However, I continued smoking weed and drinking alcohol.

During one of our rides, I finally made up my mind and said I was going to let go of my revenge. That was the worst thing I could have done. The leader was upset and said, "If we don't do something to this kid, it's going to make our crew look weak!"

I believed that God had reassured me that everything was going to be okay. I knew I couldn't explain this to my crew because they didn't go to church, and from what I could tell, they didn't have a relationship with God. All types of hell broke loose. They felt like they couldn't trust me, and they thought that I was working with the other side. They couldn't understand why I was allowing Mike to live.

I stayed away from them for about two weeks to collect my thoughts. When I finally started hanging with them again, they told me that my leader had hired another hit man to take care of me. I was amazed. They described him as a brown-skinned, heavy-set guy with curly hair. When I played dice, this guy stood next to me. A couple times, as I came out of the store, this guy was just coming in. Another time I was at a club and the guy asked me if I wanted to go to a girl's house to get high. This hitman had been in my presence all along.

I finally got tired of hiding and I came out on the block strapped. The same guy tried to play me. He came out and gave me dap. "Yo, man, you always clean. You're the coolest cat out here. Yo, Son, when I grow up I want to be just like you." Thank God, I wasn't slow. He was trying to make me drop my guard. He asked me if I could give him a ride but I told him I had somewhere to go. I played stupid, like I didn't know who he was. I knew I had to lay low and plan what to do. The block was getting hot and it seemed like it was smothering me. On one hand, I had Mike after me, and on the other hand, I had a hit man after me. I didn't realize then that God was trying to get me to surrender to Him but because of my stubbornness and anger, I didn't listen.

Around five in the afternoon, Mike showed up on the block. I had my gun, but I had left it under the porch. I was defenseless, but I had a more powerful weapon. I immediately started talking to God. All I could say was, "Jesus, help me."

Mike walked up and said, "You're about to get bodied," which meant murdered. Everybody screamed and scattered. My mind went blank, my heart was racing, but under my breath, I was talking to God, and asking Him to help me. Seemingly, out of nowhere, a car pulled up with two Italian women from a well-known family. When they pulled up, Mike already had his hands in his pants getting ready to pull out the gun. Someone screamed, "Be careful Mike, you got witnesses out here. Two girls just pulled up!" Mike walked over to their car to tell them to leave. When he turned his back, I ran.

No one can tell me God isn't real. As I look back over my life, I realize that God was with me all the time. It was time to take a break from being on the block.

Three weeks went by and I started to get comfortable not being on the block. I went back to church and began rebuilding my relationship with God. I drove around at night talking to Him. It came to me that I no longer wanted that type of life but it wasn't easy to get out of it.

• • •

One day, at six o'clock in the morning, the female I was dealing with awakened me to tell me to come look at the news. They talked about one of the biggest drug busts in the past ten years. As I watched the screen, I was amazed to see my crew being busted. I was nervous and I started thinking about what I needed to do. The reporter said the FBI was looking for several other people associated with the crew. I'd never given them my real name so no one knew it. They said that they were looking for a guy who dressed nice. I knew they were talking about me so I continued to lay low.

At least three months passed and it got quiet on the block. By then, I was more involved in the church and I had rebuilt a stronger relationship with God. I knew that He was all I had left. One day after church, I was in my friend's car at the car wash when another car pulled up next to us. My friend's window tint was dark so they couldn't see us. One of the guys got out of the car and started kicking the snow off the tires. He was smoking a blunt and talking to the other guy in the car. To my surprise, my name came up. I heard him say, "I wonder where Bless is." My friend never knew that they were talking about me because my church friends knew my real name, not my street name.

When I got home, I called my sister. She told me that there was still a contract out on me. This strengthened my belief that God was real. There's no way I should have been able to hear that conversation but evidently God wanted me to know what was going on. The Bible is true when it says He'll never leave you nor forsake you.[6]

Chapter 12

ESCAPE FROM NEW YORK

I reconnected with Andre and he told me about his plan to leave New York and move to Charlotte, North Carolina. He asked me if I wanted to go into partnership with him on a recording company. I didn't have anything else to do at the time, so I said yes.

He left me in New York with the money to rent a hotel ballroom and hold auditions. Instantly I started feeling like somebody important. I wasn't making money because I wasn't selling drugs anymore but I had a chance to be legit. I couldn't believe I was already in a position as a manager.

We put out the fliers for the audition and over thirty people applied. I didn't know anything about management, but I knew that people had to report to me. Most of the people who applied were people who hustled and because of the crew I hung with, I had earned respect, even though I didn't hang with them anymore. When people talked to me, they were nervous. Some would say, "I can't believe you went up against Mike." It made me feel like a local hero because I stood my ground.

Finally, we picked a group called the Headless Horsemen. They could really rap. The next thing we needed to do was to get them to leave New York and go to Charlotte to shoot a music video. That's where Andre came in. When he went to Charlotte, he took classes to learn how to make music videos. Sad to say, we couldn't get the group to leave New York.

One day, I was watching the news and saw a story about a guy who was murdered in gruesome fashion. The coroner described the victim as looking like Swiss cheese. Whoever killed him sat on top of him and shot him eight times in the chest and the face. There was talk on the street that this was the work of Mike. The rumors made him leave the part of New York that I was in. I felt more at peace and I didn't need to carry a gun around with me anymore.

As I continued the business with Andre, the money I had saved up was dwindling. I wasn't going to sit there and let my money blow so I went to see my cousin, Jeff, in Buffalo. When I arrived, they were partying and drinking. I was in a new city where I could smoke, drink, and party without looking over my shoulder.

I was in a club in Buffalo when my cousin came to me and told me that people in the club were asking him if I played for the Buffalo Bills. I rolled with what everybody thought and told him to say, "Yes." This was a completely new game plan for me. I was a celebrity without being a celebrity. Women flocked to me. I thought, *Wow! This is what it looks like when you're successful.* I wasn't. But hey, I rolled with it.

The following week, Jeff and I went to Toronto, Canada. It was the spitting image of New York City, but cleaner. We hit a club that held about four thousand people. The club was made up of five different music rooms. In one part of the club, there was techno. I went to another part of the club and they were playing rap, another part reggae, and another part R&B. The fifth part of the club played old school music. I could not believe it.

Back then I wore a lot of jewelry. I also had a cane and a derby hat. This was during the time a popular rapper appeared in his video wearing a cane and a derby hat and it became the fad in the streets. They didn't have anybody in Toronto that dressed like me. I was very flashy and what tipped it off was that I could really dance. I always had three or four women on the dance floor with me.

I was mesmerized by the way one particular woman looked. She was half Jamaican and half Portuguese. She was very beautiful and unique. I told her I worked for Big Boy Entertainment and the rest was history. She told all her friends that someone from Big

Boy was in the club. When the deejay played a Big Boy song, they looked at me. I would be on the dance floor dancing, singing, and profiling like I was making a music video.

After we left the club, we drove up a street where there were hundreds of women walking around. Jeff said they were prostitutes. We'd already paid for a hotel for two nights so we decided to pick up a prostitute to take back to the hotel. An Asian woman got into our car but when I looked at her, I didn't get a good feeling. Some may say I'm crazy but I still say this was God looking out for me. I asked her if she was a male or female. She said she was a female. I told her to show me. When I pulled the car over, she admitted she was a 'she-male.' I got out of the car, walked around to the side of the car where he was sitting, pulled him out of the car, then walked back to the driver's side and drove off.

Jeff had already told him what hotel we were going to in order to make 'her' feel comfortable. He had to know so he could tell his pimp. An hour later, our hotel phone rang. It was the pimp calling to tell us that we still owed him money because we picked up his girl off the street. I snatched the phone from Jeff and told the pimp if he wanted any beef, I'd be waiting in the hotel lobby. I went to the lobby in my wife beater (T-shirt) and boots. I was strapped, just hoping the pimp would show up. I waited for about forty minutes. No one ever showed.

The following night, we went back to the club and met up with two girls. We were outside and there were at least two hundred people waiting in line around the corner. I had a song playing in my head and I told Jeff and the two girls to follow me. I didn't tell Jeff what I was going to do. I put my swag on and walked through the crowd in my Gucci shoes and my Versace pants and shirt. The shirt alone cost four hundred dollars, so people knew I had money. As I walked through the crowd, I heard women saying, "He must be famous."

When we got to the door, the bouncer asked me, "Where are you going?"

I looked him in the eyes and said, "Excuse me?"

Jeff and I always did some homework before we pretended to be somebody else. It just so happened that Big Daddy was scheduled to come to that club the following week. I picked up my phone and pretended I was calling somebody. All he heard me say was, "Yeah, can I speak to James?"

The bouncer said, "Who is James?"

I said, "This is Big Daddy," pointing to my phone and acting like I was talking to Big Daddy.

I told the bouncer that I was the guy that came to check out the club before Big Daddy came to perform and I asked to speak to the manager. When the manager came out, I told him who I was. He apologized and took me straight upstairs to the VIP room. He told me to order whatever I wanted—it was on the house. I told him to bring up three bottles of Cristal and three bottles of Moët. They roped off our room and two bouncers stayed up there with us. I told the bouncers to bring women upstairs, five at a time. As the women came into the room, Jeff and I told them to walk and turn around like they were modeling on a runway. If they fit the profile, they could stay. If not, the bouncer took them back downstairs. We continued to do this until the room filled up with beautiful women.

At the end of the night, we told the girls we were getting ready to leave. They grabbed their coats and followed us. When we got to the hotel, I went to the front desk with them and asked the clerk if there were any phone calls from James 'Big Daddy' Holmes. He said, "Yes."

Now, you may be wondering, why did he say yes? That's simple. We stopped by a store and I had Jeff call the hotel acting like James 'Big Daddy' Holmes, saying he wanted me to call him right away. This was my way of balling. While other people paid to be with these women, I was getting the time, attention, and sex for free.

I enjoyed Toronto so much that I decided to move there that last month before I moved to North Carolina, but Toronto was expensive. We paid a lot for the lifestyle and glamour. Eventually, my money started running out so I went home.

Chapter 13

NEW TRICK CITY

I went back to New York but I was determined to leave for Charlotte. The word on the street was that Mike had been arrested in Brooklyn for killing the 'Swiss cheese victim.' They had so much evidence on him that I decided I wasn't leaving New York until I knew what happened to him.

On the day of his sentencing, he received two twenty-five year sentences to be served back to back. My truck was already packed and when they announced the sentence, I left New York and drove straight to North Carolina. I never looked back.

I promised myself that when I arrived in Charlotte I would be legit. I found an apartment and found a job as a hotel clerk. The apartment complex that I'd chosen did not look anything like the magazine pictures. It looked like a place that was straight from New York, the part that is heavily infested with drugs and prostitutes. When I pulled in, I saw crack heads, prostitutes, and drug dealers. I could not believe it. Here I was thinking I was escaping my past, but my past was facing me. I couldn't believe what I was seeing but one thing was different—when I woke up in the morning, it was peaceful and quiet. I heard birds chirping. I didn't hear that in New York.

The minute I went outside, there was activity going on all around me. I didn't understand the purpose of me being in the same environment I tried to escape, but I sensed in my spirit that I had to pass my test and prove to God that I was not going to go back.

My job was right down the street from where I lived so I could walk to work. I loved the job. It gave me the opportunity to mix with many different types of people.

Before I knew it, three months had passed and I had not sold drugs or committed any crimes. I would be around people who were smoking and drinking but I never participated. There were times I took the blunt in my hand and acted like I puffed it, but I didn't. After everything that happened back in New York with Mike, I told myself that I did not need to smoke or drink anymore. Occasionally, I did have a drink but it wasn't something that took me over the edge. I would still wake up the next day in my right mind. I knew the drug addiction and criminal activity was leaving me.

One afternoon while I was working at the hotel, I saw a guy who looked just like a guy I knew from New York. A few of us got away during the FBI sweep but we never told each other where we were going. We just left. He was one of them. We didn't run the streets together but we passed by each other and we spoke a lot. I never had beef with this guy but when I saw him, I was hesitant to call his name.

"Red, is that you?"

I saw him flinch. I knew he was nervous because if he was in Charlotte, he didn't want anyone to know him. To reassure him that it was safe, I walked around the counter and said, "Yo, man, what's up?"

"Hey, man. How long have you been in Charlotte?" Red asked.

"About three months."

"Yo, how's your sister? And Sasha?"

"They're fine, man. I'm at work right now, but let's hook up later," I said.

Even though we never hung out in New York, it was a relief to finally see someone I knew. We made plans to hook up and later that night, Red and some of his friends picked me up.

I didn't know the other guys he was hanging with but it was a relief to finally go somewhere. We went to a club called Vintage on the Boulevard. It was an exciting night. I felt like a brand new person. The club was small but it was very impressive. I noticed instantly that the women down south were very different from the women in New York. The women down south were thicker and shapelier. We partied all night and had a good time.

Red and me partied together for the next three months. Finally, I had someone who was more my speed. Red's brother, Shine, and me took a liking to each other and we bonded quickly. Shine started coming to pick me up throughout the day and showed me around Charlotte. We would hang out from Wednesday night until Sunday night. We always found something to do because we were both new to the Queen City. We liked to hang out in a club called CJ's in the Adam's Mark hotel. We walked into the club wearing our gator shoes and Versace suits, buying bottles of Moët and Cristal.

I realized that living in a fantasy is dangerous. I still believed that I was bigger than I actually was. I told myself that I was a pro football player from New York. I was already a video producer for Big Boy Entertainment, so why not a football player? I enjoyed experiencing the women, the clubs, and getting the best in life.

You may be asking yourself, "What would make him go this far?" I had been incarcerated and because of my record, every time I tried to get a job and go legit, I was disqualified when they saw the checked box that says, "Do you have a criminal record?" I also attended church, but it was one of the worst experiences I ever had. People talked about me behind my back and walked around me like I didn't even exist, so I said, "To hell with it. I'll do my own thing." It was survival.

What do you do when you've been raped and molested as a child and your family has put you down and considers you an outcast?

The world kept judging me because of my past and then the church that was supposed to support me and help me was the very organization that judged me the most. I'm not condoning what I did, but what do you do to survive when you feel all alone in this world?

I knew there was something special about me because even though I didn't have money and even though I didn't come from the best place, I always had ambition. I would love to have been born into a normal family, where my parents woke up every morning and said they loved me and read me bedtime stories. A family where my dad took me to the park to play ball and we all went to church together. A family where we watched movies together and we shared popcorn. A family where I got really good grades in school and I went to a major college. Unfortunately, that's not the story I can tell you.

· · ·

I hung out with my boys but I didn't have enough money to keep doing it. When my boss at the hotel gave me a raise, I was angry. I was still receiving my disability payments from the injury I sustained on the construction job in New York. I met with my boss and asked him to take back the raise. He was stunned and asked, "Are you sure?" I explained to him that I was on disability and if I made more than a certain amount, they would deduct the overage from my check. My boss took back the raise but I still needed more money. Then finally something came to me. When I was selling drugs in New York, I dealt with a crack head that put me on to a little scam he pulled on stores in the mall, especially the major department stores. I decided to try it.

The next morning when I got dressed, I wore my suit, carried my briefcase, and I went from store to store in the mall. The first week I collected fifteen hundred dollars. That went on for about a month. The next month, I got up to twenty-five hundred a week. It was almost better than selling drugs. I got a natural high. The money I had saved, plus the money from my disability check, and the money from working my scam, totaled between seven thousand to ten thousand dollars per week.

But you gotta understand ballin'. I was hanging out with ball players and the money I made wasn't a lot. I would watch one of my friends take out five hundred dollars, put it on the table, and tell the server to keep sending rounds of drinks until the money was gone. We sat there drinking all night long with women who sat at the table just to be seen with us.

One day, Shine said, "You don't really use your clothes to talk to women, do you?" He said that because there were times he would pick me up and I would just be average—no jewelry, no stylish clothes—but I still had boldness to talk to women. I never talked about money. I never talked about what I would do for them but I had confidence and I looked good. I knew that if a girl was looking for someone to be real with her, I would be that man. If I ran up on a gold digger who was always talking about money, where I was going to take her, what type of car I drove, or where I worked, I knew instantly she wasn't going to get anything from me.

I just wanted a relationship. So while we flowed on women in the mall, in the club, or at a restaurant, one thing I couldn't do was perpetrate. I couldn't talk the baller game because I wasn't going to say things like, "Let's have some shrimp, caviar, and Moët." Now it may have led up to that, but that came through me having a relationship with the woman. My friends would roll up on average women but I always picked classy women who had college degrees and wouldn't give a thug the time of day.

I'm a romantic. I'm touchy-feely. I like to rub a woman's back, play in her hair, run bath water with rose petals, and burn candles from the door all the way to the bathtub. I told my friends I didn't have to show a woman all my money. I knew if I treated her like a lady, I would win her heart. If I had the right conversation with her, I would win her mind, too.

There were late nights when women came to my house and we were sweaty from dancing and partying. I would tell them to take a shower and they would say they had nothing to put on. That wasn't a problem. I always had nightgowns and teddies from Victoria's Secret for them to wear. No matter what type of woman she was, I always had her size. When you're ballin', it's called stocking up. When I saw outfits I liked, I bought them. That was just how I was living. Everything was a go.

Chapter 14

BALLIN' AND SHOT CALLIN'

During my partying at the clubs, I met Susan. I had only dated one black woman before: Renee, the mother of my first son. I was used to dating and living with Latina women. They were sweet, but they were too nice and too loyal. Susan was black but she had a personality like the Latina girls and I liked that. The only problem was her mom. She was always talking about Susan's ex-boyfriends and it angered me. Talking about another dude is one of my triggers but I took it because I wanted to be with Susan.

After we dated for a while, she told me that she wanted to get serious. Whenever a woman said that, I tested her. I told her that she had to give up going out to the clubs, drinking, and partying. If she could do that, I knew it would only be a matter of time before *I* would give up going to the clubs. Ultimately, I wanted a wife.

Susan stuck to not going out. She went to work and then came over to my house. Even though I was still hanging out, she had dinner ready and would be awake and waiting up for me, ready to do whatever I wanted to do.

Finally, I gave in to her and I eased myself away from the club and from my friends. We started doing things together. We went to the movies or out to dinner. Sometimes we cooked dinner together at home. I felt our intimacy growing. It was great, until her friend, Carol, stepped into the picture.

Occasionally, she called to ask Susan when she was going to come by to see her. I didn't trust Carol. She was dating one of my friends but she wasn't attractive. My friend continually asked me if Susan had any friends that looked like her.

One night, I decided to hang out with my friends, just so Susan and I could have some space from each other. At the club, a woman approached me. She was beautiful and stacked in all the right places. While we were talking, a guy approached her and tried to pull her off the stool. She told him that she didn't want to go with him. We left and walked to the car but he followed us outside and tried to start a fight with her. He was talking loudly and the crowd grew larger. Then he said the wrong thing.

"What! I'm supposed to be scared of the guy you're walking with?"

I spun around. I couldn't see any of my friends, but out of nowhere Shine said, "Ain't nobody gonna jump and ain't nobody gonna do nothing."

"Yo, Shine, move aside so I can knock this dude out with one punch," I said pushing the woman behind me.

Shine said, "If you know what I mean, there won't be no licks thrown but there will be bullets flying."

The dude walked away and everybody came and gave me dap. They said, "You're the man. You made a statement tonight!" I didn't know what they meant but it felt good. It was a cool night, a light breeze was blowing, my rings were beaming, my diamond watch was glistening, my shoes were shining, and I had a woman by my side that was drop dead gorgeous. I was ballin' and shot callin' and it felt good.

The following night, Susan went to Carol's house and I hung out with my boys again. We planned to call each other at midnight, so we could meet back at the house.

As I walked into the club a dude said, "Are you Bless from New York?"

I quickly put my hands on the gun under my shirt and he said, "Yo, chill out man. It's me, Jimmy." I recognized who he was once he started talking. "What's up man? How long have you been down here?" I told him about five or six months.

He told me to come over and hang out with him and his friends. We sipped champagne, reminisced about back home, and chilled out. We partied all night and had so much fun that we decided to do it again the next night.

The following night, we went out again but I got a surprise. I was sitting there chilling out when I saw Susan come into the club. I approached her and asked her what she was doing at the club. She told me that she came with Carol, who had to check on something. I didn't know it when we met, but Carol sold weed. After I talked to Susan for a little while I said, "All right, but don't stay here too long." When you're a baller and a thug, you don't want your woman in the same place with you because you have to stand on guard to protect her, just in case someone in the club wants to act stupid.

My second surprise happened when I went back to sit with Jimmy and the boys. They said, "Yo, son, you know them?"

I said, "Yeah, that's my girl. I've been seeing her for a minute."

The entire table was silent.

"Yo, man, do you love her?" Jimmy asked.

"Nah, we just started dating. Love is a strong word."

"Well, I don't know if I should tell you this, but I gotta," Jimmy said.

My heart was racing and my palms were sweaty. I couldn't hear the music or anyone else in the club. All I heard was, "Yo, she's a freak. Her and her friend." I knew he was telling the truth but I was calm. He kept talking.

"Yo, let me tell you the truth. Listen, we had both of them in the bed together. They're dating each other."

"What?"

Jimmy said, "When we had those freaks in the bed, man, they started performing on each other."

I switched off my emotions and played it cool. We dropped the topic. I hung out with them for another hour and then I left. I was so mad that my mind was playing tricks on me. I asked myself, *is he jealous? Why would Jimmy be jealous? We were cool back home.*

I kept calling Susan's phone but I couldn't reach her, so I drove to Carol's house. When I got there, I was angry. I could see that the lights were off and I could see candles burning. I went back to the car, popped the trunk, and grabbed the gun. I tried to look through the window but I couldn't see anything.

"Susan, open up the door! Open up the door!"

Finally, Carol came to the door.

"Where's Susan?"

She didn't answer so I pushed her aside and walked into the house. Susan was sitting on the couch.

"Come on, Susan, I need to talk to you. Now!"

"She don't have to go nowhere with you," Carol said.

I pointed my gun at Carol and said through clenched teeth, "If you don't sit down and get out of my way, I know something."

"You're gonna regret pointing that gun at me," she said.

I grabbed Susan and started walking to the car. Carol came running to the car as Susan was getting in. I spun around, glared at Carol, and told her, "You make one more move to this car and I'm blasting you."

As we drove off Carol screamed, "Don't worry, you'll get yours!"

When we got back to the house, I asked Susan about what the guys had told me. She lied.

I thought about a line I'd heard in a movie, "If you can't walk away from something in thirty-seconds, you're in trouble." Well, I knew she was lying—thirty-seconds turned into forty-seconds and a minute turned into an hour. What was my problem? The same problem a lot of us have.

Sometimes you see something that's dangerous but you can't walk away. You're left feeling trapped, hurt, betrayed, and let down. After a while you say to yourself, *maybe she's telling the truth, maybe the guys are jealous.* Your conscious mind is telling you that you know it's a lie but you accept something in your life that's only going to bring you more heartache, pain, and agony.

When we got to the house, we kept arguing and I just let it all go. I was angry because she wasn't doing things my way and I was tired of her being phony.

"William, please listen to me," she said softly and seductively, attempting to manipulate me.

"Please stop! That's not the way you talk," I said.

I prayed and I hoped that we could turn our relationship around because she had the temperament that I needed, but she was more interested in impressing me than changing to save our relationship. I told her that she needed to leave. She kept trying to hug and kiss on me but I pushed her aside. What she didn't know was that I had already asked God for the strength to let her go.

I was mesmerized as I watched her walk out the door but I knew I had to be strong. I had a relationship with God and I knew I had to call on Him. He was always there. Every time a woman hurt me, I would have a sense of peace that it would be all right. I knew that once I walked away from her, I wasn't going to come back.

Chapter 15

HEARTBREAKER

As the days and weeks went by, I started working out again. I even found a church and I started attending. I decided that just like I gave my heart away to women, I would give my heart away to God. I praised Him from my heart but while I was attending church, another problem arose. I noticed a whole new breed of women that I'd never seen before—church women—all dressed up, smelling good, and looking really good. I couldn't help noticing their physical appearance, but they also had class. When I saw a classy woman, it moved me. I thought, I don't need Susan, I got girls at the church. Why do I need her?

Finally, I felt my strength coming back to me and I did what we all do after God heals our hearts. I ran back to a place that was not good for me. The Bible talks about it being like a dog returning to its vomit.[7]

I asked myself, *what is the real problem?* It was no longer the pain. It was no longer about a woman. When a woman hurt me, I worked out, got another dose of conceitedness, and became somebody brand new. I knew I would have women approaching me and lusting after me because of my physical appearance. They didn't understand what they were dealing with—someone who was looking for revenge. My working out and getting in shape became the mask that I put on to get my victims. My body was my mask. My motive was to punish women for what I had gone through. In my mind, all women were the same.

I decided that I was no longer going to date women to fall in love with them. It was time to become an all out heartbreaker. I went back to the clubs and instantly I became the man. I felt good and I still had money. It felt like good times again but every classy woman I saw in the club brought back memories of Susan. My heart raced and I felt tense.

I practiced what I would say to Susan if I saw her again, but when I finally did see her, my feelings for her were gone.

• • •

I had less than three months before my lease was up. In those three months, I drifted back into hanging out. It was subtle at first. I called Shine and he came and picked me up. I didn't have that much money but I still went to the clubs and had fun.

One night, I met a German woman. Her name was Nadia. She asked me what I did for a living and I told her I played pro football. She was very impressed. It's funny how women would give themselves to me as long as I was in shape and they thought I had money. My arms were visibly hard and they could see them and touch them. That turned them on.

Men are fascinated by how thick a woman is or if she has long hair. Women are fascinated by what a man is driving or what type of job he has. Here I was with no job and receiving lifetime disability—no real substance. I was thugging, bugging, lying, stealing, and ex-drug dealing. All I had were my looks and my gift of gab. I remember walking into those clubs and hearing women say, "Mm...mmm...mmm," when they saw me.

I talked to Nadia until she finally wanted to go back to my place. I didn't have hotel money so I needed to come up with something quick. Football season was several months away. I finally told her that I had just been traded and I'd only been in town for two months. I told her that when you've been traded due to injury, they don't give you your money and your bonus up front. I told her that the team bought apartments and let players stay there free, but it was on a first come, first served basis. I told her that the apartment I had was probably one of the worst. What could I say? It was free. I told her that I only had one month to stay there but the minute that training camp started I'd be getting seven and a half million dollars. Once I signed, I would start working out with the team and prove that I could still play ball after my injury. The next question was about my car. I told her that my car was in the shop. Then I told her that even though I was staying in the apartment, I was building a brand new house at the lake.

The furniture in my apartment wasn't the best because my furniture, my money, and my car were tied up in New York and were not being released to me. The bedroom suite I had was definitely not impressive. Nadia became leery as the alcohol wore off. Then she said, "You're gonna have to prove to me that what you're telling me is the truth."

I said, "No problem. Let's take a drive and I'll show you the car and the house." I remembered that my friends showed me a dealership on South Boulevard that sold exotic cars so we headed that way.

When we arrived, we got out to go look at the cars. I'm thinking and I'm walking. I'm thinking and I'm walking. I'm thinking and I'm walking. Finally, the plan came to me. There was an S430 Mercedes Benz on the lift in the repair area. I told her it was mine and they were checking it out because I had problems with the tires. She was amazed and said, "Wow! That's a nice car." I couldn't believe that she believed it but she did. The reason she believed it was because I told her to stay in the car and I walked around and made sure everything was okay. As I walked back I said, "Now what did they do with my platinum car?" I said stuff like, "I know they didn't leave my car out here in this weather."

After that, she was determined to see the house that I was building before we could go back to my place. I remembered my friend taking me out to Lake Norman and showing me some houses. I couldn't remember much about the place but I remembered the exit, and once I got to the exit, I remembered how to get to the housing development where there were million dollar homes. When we got to the subdivision, I picked out a house. As we walked to the porch I prayed, "Lord, please let this door be unlocked."

To my surprise, I turned the doorknob and it was unlocked. Once the door opened, I acted like I was a realtor and we went into the house. It had spiral staircases, three levels, and an elevator. I described each room and as I pointed I said, "This will be ours and this is where you will be." That was all she wrote. She was mine and all it took was the promise of a car and a house that weren't even mine.

• • •

That summer I moved to the East side of town. Charlotte reminded me a little bit of New York boroughs. When I moved from the South side to the East side, it was a very different atmosphere with different people and different scenery. There was more to do. I felt like a brand new person that nobody knew. The guys from the church continued picking me up in the church van because I didn't have a vehicle. The van driver told me that they could pick me up for the rest of the month and then I would have to find an apartment closer to church. Once they stopped coming to pick me up, I stopped going to church. I sat at home and watched Christian broadcasts on television. I didn't know too much about the East side, so I didn't know about a church on that side of town. The friends that I knew from back home didn't live that far from me so I saw my friend Shine more often. That slowly pulled me back into going out.

I continued calling my attorney in New York to see when the money from my disability settlement would be released. I was running low on funds, so I told him that I wanted a lump sum settlement. While I waited for the settlement, Shine asked me about going to a bike rally in Myrtle Beach. I told him I wanted to go. I still had some money saved up but I wasn't going to touch it. I didn't want to go broke.

I knew I needed money so I went back to my old trick of making money by going to the mall. The bike rally was the following week and I made about twenty-five hundred dollars on the mall scam. We rented a beach house and it was laid out. All I could hear was the sound of motorcycles riding up and down the street.

I walked on the strip and there was a spirit of lust all around me. Women were walking around in bikinis and G-strings. I couldn't believe my eyes. At the same time, my flesh was enticed. Guys were video taping women wearing their bikinis and riding on the backs of bikes. People were walking around smoking weed and drinking alcohol and beer. The women were nearly naked.

When I finally realized that the beach was beautiful, my mind instantly went into a romantic state. I told Shine, "I'm going to find a nice woman. We're going to go to the beach at night with a bottle of champagne, grapes, and blankets and chill out on the beach." He laughed and said, "Good luck with that. You won't find that down here. Man, these women come down here to have a good time. Romance is not on their radar." I kept hope alive until I met a few women and asked what they were doing later that night. They instantly asked me if I owned a bike and I knew that my romantic plans were a wrap.

One day, I finally lucked up. I met a girl and we chilled and talked. She had the same thing on her mind as I did. We didn't get to grab the wine and grapes but we did lay out on the beach. Nothing sexual happened. It was just a comfortable feeling. I decided I would go to the beach more often, but not during bike week.

Old feelings of being in a lasting relationship came back to me but they only lasted for a minute. I was too afraid to put my heart back into love again. I didn't trust women.

When we got back to Charlotte, I continued collecting my disability checks, I worked out, and I delved deeper into the Bible. Even though I was building myself up spiritually, I was losing financially. The big payment I was waiting for from the settlement had not come through yet. I needed money and I needed it fast, so I continued pulling my mall scam. I came out with another fifteen hundred dollars a week.

The sales people started asking me questions and that made me nervous. It seemed like everything was closing in on me but I continued pulling my scam. This time I picked a major hardware store. It was a bit more dangerous but it worked. The financial return was greater.

One day, my friends and I met up with these Asian girls. I told them that I was an NFL pro football player. The girls were excited and they asked me if I could get them tickets to a game. I picked up the phone, pretended like I was calling one of my team members, and told him to meet me the next day to bring some tickets for the girls. My friend laughed and said, "Man, are you still pulling that?"

We went out with the girls and had fun but for some reason I was not feeling good in my spirit. I was getting tired of that game. We went out the next night and I found myself in the club drinking, but talking to God at the same time. I didn't know what was happening. It seemed as if that part of my life was coming to an end.

Chapter 16

MARRIAGE 101

One night we went to the club and there she was . . . standing in the corner. She had long black hair and beautiful skin. When I saw her, everything around me came to a halt. I could no longer hear the music or see the crowd of people. All I saw was her. I tapped my friend and said, "Yo, son, do you see that?"

There were several guys already trying to talk to her but I said to myself, *I gotta have her. I need to come up with something to get her attention.* One of the guys said she was from France. My mind was racing. I finally approached her and introduced myself as Javier. I told her that I was a modeling agent. She told me her name was Antoinette and we exchanged phone numbers.

Just when I felt like I was ready to give up the lying and deceit, I was pulled right back in. I didn't call her for a couple of days because I wanted to string her along. She fell right into my hands and called me repeatedly. On the third day, I finally returned her call. I told her that I was in California doing a video shoot. We made plans to meet that Saturday afternoon.

When I called Shine and told him that I was going to meet the French girl, he didn't believe me. I rented a car, wore my finest clothes, picked up Shine, and then we picked her up. After I dropped him off, Antoinette and I went to get something to eat and then we went shopping and dancing. I bought her shoes and a dress and then took her back to my place so she could get dressed there. She already had a bag packed. I didn't know anything about her but I had to have her. The devil always knew what to throw at me.

We went out and had a good time, and within two weeks, I moved her in with me. I felt like I had died and gone to heaven. We went to the movies together, took long walks in the park, and walked through the mall holding hands. I had finally found someone to romance.

After a month passed, she told me that she was from France but had come to North Carolina from Miami. She said that she ran away from France because her dad sexually abused her. That explained her sexual appetite. She could never get enough when we were together.

One night, I left Antoinette at home while I went out to party. I had a bottle of Alizé at the house that I never touched. When I returned, my house had been torn apart. She came out of the room staggering and I saw that the bottle was empty. She was crying, throwing stuff, and saying that men were no good. I told her she had to get herself together, pack her stuff, and leave. Then she told me she was in trouble. I didn't believe her until she made a call and I could hear a guy on the other end speaking in Spanish. He was a Colombian.

She told me that she'd met some Colombians in Miami and she had robbed them. They were in Charlotte looking for her, but they couldn't find her because she was staying with me. I immediately helped her pack her stuff, dropped her off at a friend's house, and told her to never return to my place. I told her that I had ways of finding the Colombians and delivering her right to them. After I dropped her off, I stayed in a hotel for about a week, just in case she came back to my place and brought the Columbians there.

• • •

As I continued my search for money, I called Shine. I hadn't seen him in six months but we decided to go into business together. We opened a car dealership but it just didn't seem right. Then one day, he came in and he was sweating, saying that he needed a ride.

While I was driving, I noticed he had a knapsack and I asked him, "What's the problem, Shine?"

"Yo, Son, just keep driving. Do you see any cars following us?" he asked, while looking at the side view mirrors.

"I see a blue car. What's up, Shine? What the hell is going on?"

"Yo, there's Feds in that car."

"Aw man, you gotta be kidding me! Yo, man, why'd you get in my car? What's in the bag?" I said while weaving through traffic.

"Half a key of coke."

I started praying. I asked God to forgive me and to let me get away. I pleaded with God and told him that if I got out of there He didn't have to worry about me pulling any scams or associating with any criminal activity again.

I changed lanes and the blue car did the same. I drove past a moving company and a truck was getting ready to pull out but the driver let me pass. The FBI car was behind me but the truck pulled out right after I passed it and blocked the Feds. That gave me enough time to turn the corner. I told Shine to grab his knapsack and jump out.

The blue car caught up to me, pulled me over, and the agent told me to get out of the car. He asked me where was the other man in the car and I told him, "Sir, I don't know. The guy jumped out of the car." The agent jumped back in his car and sped off trying to catch him. I never saw Shine again.

I thank God to this day. God was the only reason that I beat a thirty-nine-year to life sentence for running drugs.

• • •

I went back to pulling my mall scam. Then one day I returned a comforter to the store and the serial numbers on the comforter didn't match the receipt. I was arrested, I received a ticket, and I had to go to court. I told the judge that I bought the comforter from someone on the street and returned it to the store. They put me on probation and charged me with a fine.

FROM HELL TO GRACE

My probation officer was cool. He often asked me why I was even in his office. We laughed and we joked every time I reported to him. I came in one day and he said he wanted me to meet someone. She was a friend of his and she was a probation officer, too. We all started hanging out and I thought, *look at me. I committed a crime and now I'm dating a probation officer.*

One night she stayed at my place and I forgot to turn my answering machine down. About three o'clock in the morning, Antoinette called. She was crying and begging me to pick up the phone so we could talk. This went on until six in the morning. My new girl and I argued all night.

We continued dating but there was one problem—she was very controlling. One morning she watched me doing my devotions and said, "You're scaring me. I didn't know I was dealing with a preacher man." I told her that I wasn't a preacher man but I did have a relationship with God.

Later, I found out that she was dating me just to get back at another guy. When I found out I was devastated and I was hurt. There I was thinking about settling down again. I had given up hanging out with my friends and even pulling my scams. I finally pulled away but I was left with devastation in my heart and I felt emptiness in my spirit.

I really didn't want to steal anymore. I didn't want to lie anymore. At times, I separated myself from everybody to be in the presence of God. When I was with Him, I felt goose bumps and an overwhelming sense of peace came over me.

• • •

Finally, my lawyer contacted me to tell me that the money I was waiting for was on its way. I was excited! After fees, I wound up with sixty-four thousand dollars. It was a hot Friday afternoon and the mail ran after five o'clock. With a big check in my hand, all I could think about was cashing it. I did something that I still regret. I called a check-cashing place. When I cashed the check, they couldn't give me the whole amount. They told me that they would give me part of the money but I would have to come back on Monday for the rest. I told them it was fine because I didn't want to go into the weekend without having my money.

I went crazy. I bought more diamond rings, designer watches, clothes, and a brand new car with cash. I went to the club with my cousin and we were so wasted that I lost twenty-five hundred dollars. I never found the money but I told my cousin that the next night I was gonna come out and have double the money. I dipped into the stash, got more money, and went to hang out, but hanging out and partying didn't feel the same. I felt in my spirit that I needed to settle down. I didn't want to waste the money in the street so I found a job and started working. I furnished my house with the cash.

One day while I was out shopping, I met Donna. She was short, light-skinned, and had black hair. She fit the profile of every woman I'd dated in the past. She told me that she was a model and a makeup artist and that she traveled frequently. We exchanged numbers and I called her the next day on my way to work.

She laughed and said, "What are you doing calling me so early in the morning?" I told her I had thought about her all night. We laughed and giggled on the phone until she told me that she was getting ready to go to school. The fact that she was in school impressed me even more.

We started hanging out. When she came to my house to do her homework, I sat with her and massaged her back and her shoulders while she worked. We were dating for about a month when we started talking about marriage. She was into church already and I was happy about that. I met her family and everything seemed okay. I had everything I needed. Everything was paid for. I just needed a wife. The funny thing about having money is that you start leaving God out of it. I wasn't doing my devotions. I wasn't praying. I thought I could just buy the things I wanted and I no longer had to wait on God.

Donna and I got married after dating only three months. Her mom said it was too fast but we didn't listen. We went to the Justice of the Peace and got married. Then all hell broke loose.

I came home from work one day and Donna wasn't home. I called her but I didn't get an answer. I went by her mom's house and they told me they hadn't heard from her either. Finally, Donna called me at eight o'clock that night. She told me that after she got off work, she went out with some of her college friends and that she couldn't call me because her phone was dead. I knew that was a lie but I couldn't prove anything.

I started praying for discernment again and found a church for us to attend. I thought that since I was married and I had everything I wanted, I could finally sell my heart out to God. I was wrong. We started attending church together and immediately she said that she didn't like the church.

Yeah, isn't that backwards? This is what we do—we make all the arrangements and then we want God to bless our mess. God was nowhere in that marriage. God kept telling me that He was going to protect me but I didn't know what He meant.

I continued fasting and praying for my marriage even though it was not going well. I knew that my reason for marrying Donna was not biblical at all. There were times the marriage was okay but then there were times when it was disastrous. Every time I went to her mom's house for dinner or a visit, she always brought up one of Donna's ex-boyfriends. Her mom also attacked me when I didn't give her money. I thought that the marriage was payback for the way I had treated women in my past.

Eventually, she started coming home late from work. Her mom said that she was out with her sister. So the next time she was late, I parked my car at a distance from her house and waited. An hour later, the car pulled up and another man was driving. Donna got out and went into the house. I jumped out of my car and banged on the door. Within ten minutes, there were five police cars there. They told me that her mother called the police and wanted me to stay away from her house. I told them that my wife was upstairs and I wanted to speak with her. The police officer rang the doorbell and told her mother that I needed to speak with Donna. Then the officer went inside. Later, he came out to tell me that Donna didn't think it was a good idea for her to come home because I was upset. I left.

The following morning she came home, changed into her work clothes, and said that we would talk later. She apologized and said that one of her college friends came to visit her and they hung out. She told me that the guy who was driving was her sister's boyfriend. I asked her why she was in the front seat of the car and she said that her sister was drunk and needed to lay in the back seat. Something in my spirit told me she was lying. I continued asking but she kept saying that she was telling the truth.

We were supposed to go on a cruise for our honeymoon but I told her that I wasn't going on a cruise with her until I found out the truth. She stuck to her version of what happened and I told her that what she was saying was not what was in my spirit. She left that night and said she wouldn't go on the cruise because she didn't want to ruin my time.

The next morning, I was on a flight to Miami with both of our tickets. When I boarded the ship, a member of the crew asked if my wife was joining me. I told him no. Everywhere I looked, I saw happy couples walking around together. I walked around the ship and eventually found my room.

When I opened the door, Donna was sitting on the bed. I was stunned, amazed, and happy at the same time. I asked her how she got on the ship and how she got on the plane. She told me that she called the airline and told them she overslept and missed her flight. She told them she was supposed to go on a cruise with her husband for our honeymoon and they immediately put her on the next available flight. I still wondered how she got on the ship because I had her ticket. She said that when she arrived the captain pulled up the passenger list to confirm she was supposed to be traveling with me. He agreed to give her an hour to find me so I could give her the ticket.

Before I gave her the ticket, I told her that we had to talk because I was not going to enjoy myself until she confirmed what was in my spirit. She said she'd been up all night talking to God and God told her if she wanted the marriage to work, she had to tell me the truth. She told me to have a seat and what happened next blew my mind. She told me that she had an affair with the guy who I'd caught her with in the car. I was so upset that my first thought was to throw her overboard.

God instantly spoke to my spirit. He reminded me of the married women I had been involved with and of the women I had dated who were already in relationships. That was His way of showing me that as He forgave me, I needed to forgive Donna. Immediately, I did exactly what God put on my spirit and I forgave her.

It was a seven-day cruise. We argued until I couldn't take it anymore. I called the captain and told him I needed some time to myself. He said they had a spare room on the ship where I could stay. I cried. I was hurt, alone, and devastated. What was supposed to be a nice honeymoon turned out to be a miserable trip.

When we got home, I set up an appointment for us to talk to Pastor Gates at Vision Christian Center. On the morning of the appointment, Donna said that she didn't want to meet with Pastor Gates. She claimed her family had left the church because of things they knew about him and his wife. I told her that was fine and that I would find another counselor we could talk to.

A week passed and then someone told me about University Church. I went to visit the church on that Sunday and the sermon touched me. On Monday morning, I looked in the phone book for the pastor's phone number. I called and told him my story. He told me that God had something great for me but he wanted me to speak to one of his associates, Pastor John H. Jamison. He told me to talk to him and he would be able to help me because he heard from God.

I called that afternoon and set up the appointment for that Wednesday. Donna agreed to meet me at University Church at one o'clock but she never came. I decided I would still meet with Pastor Jamison.

I explained our problems to him. I was in tears and I remember him saying, "Young man, you have a call on your life." I didn't know what that meant but I'd heard it before. He gave me his card and I put it in my pocket. He also told me that I had to be rooted in a church. I was so devastated, so hurt, and so lost. Life didn't make sense anymore. Donna went to stay at her mom's house for a while. She said that she was sorry she had hurt me but she couldn't bear to see me living through the pain.

One afternoon I heard a knock at the door. I thought it was Donna but when I looked through the peephole, I was surprised to see a sheriff's deputy. When I opened the door, he gave me papers for a restraining order and told me I had to go to court. I asked him to explain, and as I was talking, he stopped me and asked if I was a minister. I told him no. He told me that I needed to find a church because I had a call on my life and that I needed to trust God when I went to court. Later, when I talked to Donna, she apologized and said that her mom made her do it.

That weekend, Donna and her parents showed up at the house to get all her stuff. I pleaded with her not to leave. My throat, my voice, and my heart dropped as I watched her pack her belongings and walk out the door.

On Monday morning, I went to court with confidence. She never showed up and the judge dropped the case.

Chapter 17

SELF-RELIANCE

The month after Donna left, I lost forty pounds. I couldn't sleep in the bed because of the memories, so I slept on the floor. Mentally, I was gone.

Within six months, I had gone from having sixty–four thousand dollars to having only two thousand dollars in the bank. I had paid for the cruise, the furniture, diamond rings, diamond watches, and my car with cash. I had stuff but I didn't have money.

It seemed like everything I did wrong was ending. I didn't know what I was going to do. Until one day, I met these women from New York. They told me they could make up a resume for me. I gave them my name and that's all they asked for. They took care of everything else by themselves. They wrote me up as a senior collections manager. I went home, studied information about collections, and tried to learn the lingo. Then I started sending out the resumes. I was getting calls left and right. Sometimes in the interview, I didn't even know what I was saying. I thank God for a quick mind. Yeah, I know I shouldn't be thanking God for doing something evil but I'm thanking Him for giving me a sharp mind and the ability to use it quickly. I was just using it for the wrong purpose.

The jobs I took paid me good money. The easy part was getting on the phone, letting the computer dial the number that came up, and asking people about a loan or a bill that was not paid. The hard part was using the computer to type in customer data. I didn't have any computer skills and I was often stuck. However, that wasn't the only issue.

I had been working on a job for two days when they called me into the office and told me they had to let me go. It was not due to my performance but it was because my background check had finally come back. Even though the charges on my record were more than five years old, they still had to let me go.

I was frustrated and I told God that every time I tried to do well I was knocked back down. This time I was determined to push forward and not fall back into crime. I thought often about what might have happened to my wife, Donna, if we had stayed together. I realized that because I took matters into my own hands without consulting God, I was reaping what I sowed. I battled in my mind about the marriage and how it could have been better if I had done it the right way.

I continued putting out my resume and I got an interview at a bank for a collections position. The day of the interview I sat at a table with four people interviewing me at the same time. Talk about intimidating. They said they were so impressed by the resume that they had to talk to me. During the interview, I talked about the drug game but just switched up the words. I talked about my experience working with a large company. When people owed them money, I called them, but I told them it was a little different in New York. We would also have someone go by their job, their home, and even the ballpark if we had to. They wanted to hear how it worked and if it was dangerous. I had them eating out of my hands.

One woman said, "Yes, we do the same thing here but we would never think to send our employees out in the street."

I responded, "Yes, I know. But in New York, you have to be a go-getter."

This statement sold like hotcakes because none of them knew anything about New York. They were born and raised in Charlotte. One guy asked me if I was ever scared. I told him that I had to eat. I told them if I collected on a loan of half a million, then I would get about five percent of that. Boy, did that impress them!

Then they asked me what was the largest amount of money I ever made for a company. I sat across from them with my foot shaking under the table and twirling my fingers. I said I made about two million in fewer than nine months. Everyone at the table raised their eyebrows and became silent. Before I could open my mouth, they got up, shook my hand, and told me the job was mine. One of the guys said, "If you made two million in nine months, we can only imagine what you can do for this company your first year."

They told me to stay put and then they stepped out of the room. When they returned, they told me that not only was the job mine, but they also felt good about me and they were going to give me the lead position over the entire collections department. The job I'd applied for was paying $50,000 a year but the position they offered me paid $65,000 a year.

Now life is funny. We praise God for something He had nothing to do with because God does not succumb to evil. Out of habit, I thanked Him anyway. They told me they could start me right away and their background check would take about a month. Since I was from New York, they were willing to take a chance on me. I thought that was great. It gave me a month to make some good money.

Then it happened—they wanted me to take a test. There were questions about collections and math problems that I had never seen before. I looked over the paper and my hopes went down. About twenty minutes later, the guy came back into the room and asked me if I was finished. I told him I needed a little more time and he said, "Take your time. I'm sure with your skills you'll probably get every last problem right." He said that I had to get at least seventy percent correct.

After the guy left, I waited another five minutes and then crept out of the room. I had to go past the receptionist and I had my briefcase in my hand. I told her my parking meter was about to run out and she said, "No problem. We can validate your parking for you." I told her my parking ticket was in the car and she said,

"Oh, you can wait until you finish taking the test." I told her I had to go downstairs and get something anyway.

When I finally heard the elevator sound, it was the best sound I had ever heard. I jumped on the elevator and made my way from the seventh floor to the first floor. I spoke to the security guard, jumped in my car, and I was gone.

I got a call for another job but when they put me in front of a computer, I didn't even know where the power button was located. I realized that being street smart and book smart are two different things. The woman came in, turned on the computer, and got me started. I was embarrassed but the truth is—I just didn't know.

I had dyslexia and unfortunately, my parents never did anything when the teachers wrote notes to let them know I needed extra help. One doctor finally explained to me that people who suffer from learning disabilities may be challenged in some areas, but gifted in others. We often make mistakes in life when we laugh at the way someone speaks, spells, or reads. It's as though we're saying that their life is meaningless and ours are not. However, stop and ask yourself, who created them? The answer is the almighty God. I love the scripture in the Bible where God says He will take the foolish things of the world to conform the world.[8]

I went through life being laughed at, picked on, and never chosen to be on anybody's team—all because I didn't fit the profile. This created a state of self-reliance. When we do not regard people as equals, the only thing we're doing is sending these people, especially our teenage boys, back into a world of crime and becoming a high school dropout. I wish I had someone who took the time to sit alongside me and talk to me—someone who wanted to learn about the many things that took place in my life instead of judging me first.

Chapter 18

TRYING TO FLY STRAIGHT

I went home and asked God what I could do after years of being in the street. God put on my spirit that when I was in New York I had little jobs, but at the time, I didn't think they were important. Those jobs were working with kids. I mean just as clear as day, I heard God say, *"Children."* I went to the store right away and bought a newspaper to look at the classified ads. I looked for any job that was hiring to work with kids. I came across a job in a group home. I interviewed, got the job, and started working. Many of the kids there reminded me of myself—kids who had been abused, neglected, or molested. They had issues that brought on mental challenges and they needed my help.

I loved going to work and the kids loved seeing me. The job was exciting. It finally made me feel like I was part of something good but I continued running into problems with staff members. They used the company van for their personal use, which left me at the home having to use my personal car to take the kids out. There were times when we had an outing planned with the kids and I had to use my personal vehicle. Without thinking or even using wisdom, I used the company gas card. I assumed it would be okay because it was part of the schedule to take the kids out. I didn't know too much about the group home's protocol or standard procedures because that was my first real job.

At one of our staff meetings, the managers asked about the van being gone so long. I didn't want to snitch so I went down with everyone else and faced the consequences. Where I come from, snitching is not an option. However, I did tell them that because the van was not on the premises, I had to use my car. They told me that was fine. I forgot to tell them that I also used the gas card.

A couple weeks later when the billing came out, they called me in the office and asked me about the card. They told me that using the gas card for my personal vehicle was unacceptable. They told me I should have contacted them. I reminded them that they never gave me their phone numbers and none of the other staff members had their numbers either. They told me to go back to work.

Within an hour, they posted their emergency contact information and procedures. When I saw the posting, I thought to myself, *what is this about?* I worked that day but the next day they called me to come in early. I had to meet with the owner and he told me that they could no longer keep me because I used the credit card. I explained to him about not having emergency contact information but he said that he saw the numbers posted. I told him they had just posted them, and right in my face the managers said that they didn't do it.

I couldn't believe it. I stayed there pleading with the owner and telling him that it wasn't true, but it didn't make a difference. He told me he still had to let me go. I told the kids that I was no longer going to be working with them and they cried. Many of them hugged me and begged me not to go. It took everything in me not to cry in front of them because I'd become so attached to them. After that day, I stayed in the bed for a whole week. I was depressed. I'd finally found something that I really liked to do. I really loved the kids and my job was taken away from me. The devil pestered me to go back and pull another scam.

As I walked into the store, I could feel the pain in my heart. One of the workers was excessively excited and asked me if I was there to make a return. I told her yes and she told me to wait because she didn't have enough money in the register. She went to the back of the store and I followed her. I heard her on the phone with the police saying, "Briefcase and suit guy is here." My heart started racing.

When she turned around and saw me, I told her I had to use the bathroom. She told me that the bathroom was around the corner. I went to the bathroom but I had to think of something quickly. As I walked back to the counter, I saw the manager. I already knew what was going on. I told the manager that I had more stuff in the trunk and asked him if I could go and get it. He said it was okay.

I went outside, ducked behind some cars, eased into my car, and drove off. I drove home, took off my suit, and put regular clothes on, not knowing if they were going to come to the house looking for me. The scheming gig was over. It had been a good two–year stretch but that chapter was definitely closed.

• • •

I went out to the club one night and met a woman named Maria. We danced, we talked, and we exchanged numbers. I called her the next day and she came over that afternoon, but we weren't alone. She brought her mother with her. We continued dating and hanging out. She was sweet, kind, and caring but I realized in the midst of our relationship that I still had rage, anger, and jealousy problems. I hadn't gotten over the stuff that happened to me with other women.

Because of her temperament, Maria was too friendly with men. She had the gift of mercy, which caused her to not use wisdom at times. She told me about a guy at her job that she had lunch with and before I knew it, I was yelling and screaming.

She called me the next morning before she went to work and she apologized. Because I wasn't working at the time, I was taking her daughter to daycare. She asked me if I was still going to take her daughter to school. When I went to pick up her daughter, Maria apologized again. I felt so bad that I still had the anger problem. I know that there is such a thing as being protective, but I was a walking time bomb. I was the one who had lost their temper, and she was still the one apologizing to me.

Another time when she and I were arguing, she hung up on me after saying awful things to me. I went to her house and used the key that she had given me but she had put the second lock on the door. I banged on the door and shouted at her to let me in. I had a flashback of when I went to Donna's house and they wouldn't open the door. I snapped and I kicked the door in. She was sitting on the couch with her daughter and her son. The kids were screaming and Maria was shouting, "Don't hit me! My kids are right here!"

I didn't hit her but I did scream and yell at her. I told her not to ever lock me out again. Locking me out or walking away from me made me think of the rejection of my family, my friends, and my ex-wife.

The worst incident happened when her niece wanted to come over. I told her that I didn't care if the girl came over but there could be no smoking weed, no drinking, and no guys in the house around the kids. I really protected those kids. I made sure that they always watched kid friendly shows—nothing with profanity and nothing sexual.

Maria used to work a lot and by the time she came home, I'd already picked the kids up from school and cooked dinner. I remember going into the daycare and a few of the daycare workers said to me, "Sir, I tell you this—the woman that you got is very lucky. The little boy told us that you're not his dad but he cares for you. Every time you show up I notice the little girl runs to you." They were telling me that I was a good man but I didn't feel like one. I felt like the Incredible Hulk.

That night, I fell asleep after talking to Maria on the phone. When I woke up it was almost midnight. I was furious that I slept for almost four hours and she didn't even call me to check on me and wake me up. I woke up thinking that she and her niece must be at her house having a good old time. I got up, grabbed my gun, and went to her house.

I put the key in the door with one hand and I had my gun in the other hand. The minute I opened the door I smelled weed throughout the house. I went into the kids' room and her niece was stretched out in the bed with an empty beer bottle on the floor, blunts rolled up with weed, an ashtray, and a condom wrapper beside the bed. That was it! My mind was gone! Instantly I thought that both of them must have had this going on. I had warned Maria and I'd told her that I didn't want this kind of stuff going on around the kids.

I crept into her room, woke her up, and told her I needed to talk to her. She sat up in the bed and asked what was wrong. I told her to get out the bed so we could talk in the TV room. I did this because the kids were in her bed with her. She followed me to the TV room. I turned around and showed her my gun. I shouted, "Don't ever play with me again. You got your niece having sex in the next room, you got your kids in here, and marijuana smoke is all through the house. The next time it happens, I will come through and make sure I clear the house." I knew I was angry, but not angry enough to use the gun on her. After my years of gang banging, that life made me treat a woman the same way I treated a man if I felt betrayed. The gun was always the answer.

She cried and said, "Okay, okay. I'm sorry. I won't do it again."

Looking at her made me sick. I couldn't believe what I had done. She didn't deserve that. Every time I thought someone betrayed me, I turned violent.

One day while I was at work, Maria called and told me that her mother's boyfriend called and said he was going to come over so they could have a drink. My mind was frenzied. I asked for his number, then I called him and told him that if he asked her to have a drink with him again, he was going to have problems with me. He threatened me, called me a punk, told me he didn't care what I said, and hung up the phone. I had ten more minutes before I was off work and those last few minutes went by slowly.

I got off work and called him but he wouldn't answer the phone. I called Maria and asked her if he came over. She said no, but he did call and tell her what he would do to me. I hung up the phone with her and I called her mother. I told her mother what took place and she said she had not seen him. I told her he had ten minutes to give me a call and if he didn't, I was coming over to her house to shoot it up. She called her daughter and told her what I said. Maria knew that I was going to do it so she called and pleaded with me not to. It didn't make a difference. She thought that he wanted to come over for an innocent drink but I knew there was more behind it.

Seven minutes went by and my phone rang. He was on the other end of the phone with her mother, pleading with me not to come over to the house. He apologized and said he was drunk and didn't know what he was saying. I told him that he didn't have to worry about me shooting up the house but he was gonna have to see me. I told him that if he didn't want me to come to the house, I would give him a spot and a time he needed to meet me.

As I was driving over there to meet him, Maria called me and pleaded with me not to go. She said that he was scared and he said he would never call her again or try to come over there when I wasn't there.

What he did instantly triggered memories of me being molested. All I thought about was him going over there, getting her drunk, and taking advantage of her or her kids. I was looking for revenge for my lost childhood. I could hear the devil talking to me, telling me what I needed to do, and I was going to do it. Maria was on the phone crying, telling me how much she loved me and didn't want me to do anything stupid. Because of the hurt I had already caused her, I let her words sink in as she pleaded with me to come home.

I called him back and told him that he'd better count his blessings. He thanked me and told me if I ever needed anything from him to just let him know. I told him I didn't need anything from him but if he ever thought to pick up the phone and call my girl-friend again, that it would be the last time. I was so serious that I tasted blood in my mouth.

My mind was tormented from everything that I'd been through as a child. There were times I didn't know if I was coming or going or if I wanted to live or die. I couldn't share this with anybody so I kept silent. I was like a wild man wishing I could control the beast within.

Eventually, we started going to church as a family and I was proud of myself that several months went by and I never lashed out at Maria again. As I think about it now, part of her staying with me was love and part of it was her own insecurities.

• • •

One day while I was on my way home from work my phone rang. It was my ex-wife, Donna. I hadn't heard from her in close to a year. She asked how I was doing and told me that I sounded different. I asked her why I could never find her. She told me that the week after she left she moved to Florida. She said her mom made her do it. I told her that was fine and I hoped all was well. Then she told me the other reason why she picked Florida. You could live there less than a year and get a divorce. She let me know that the divorce papers would be coming in the mail and that her mother was going to meet me to sign them and have them notarized. She would then give them to Donna to send them off.

I hadn't seen her mother in nine months, but I walked into the bank, got the papers notarized, shook her hand, and tried to be the better person by asking her to forgive me for any hurt I may have caused. She said, "William, don't worry about it. You and Donna only dated for three months before you rushed into marriage, and that caused many problems." She was right. I probably would have been excessively protective, too, if I had a child that married someone after knowing him or her for only three months.

Maria and I continued dating. I was a better person. I had a girlfriend, I loved her kids, and we had a family. I was still going to church although Maria was not going anymore. Her mother and I became friends because she saw me striving to go to church to make my life better. When she asked me about Maria, I said, "Ma'am, she stayed home." Maria and I never lived together. I had my own place and she had her own place but we stayed at each other's place from time to time.

When Valentine's Day came around, we wanted to get away. We decided to go to Myrtle Beach. We rented a car and before we could even get out of the driveway, someone sideswiped us. I felt in my spirit that maybe it was not meant for us to go. After the police came, the car rental company gave us another vehicle and we drove to the beach. We argued the entire trip.

When we returned to Charlotte, I started staying home, reading the Bible more, and turning down having sex with her and sleeping over at her place. She accused me of seeing someone else. What she didn't know is that someone else was Jesus.

There were also problems with her not being able to stand on her own two feet without letting her mom manipulate her. As a man, that was something I couldn't allow. It made me feel like she was weak and she wouldn't be able to stand up for me with her family. We needed a break.

Chapter 19

I STOPPED CALLING AND HE DIED

I found a job at a car dealership in Charlotte. It was my ninth job within a year. The guys I worked with carried their guns inside the car dealership. They said things like, "Jim (the manager), did you make sure you brought your gun inside? Just in case these people in Charlotte start acting up." and "No disrespect to y'all but we heard Charlotte was wild." All the other salesmen were 'do boys.' They would bow down and 'do' whatever they were told to do. Some of them said, "I ain't trying to make them mad and get shot."

It made me angry and I didn't know if they were crazy enough to try anything so I brought my gun to work and hid it in my suit jacket. I told one of the salesmen that I had it and I even showed him the gun when we went to lunch. When we came back from lunch, the manager said he needed to speak to me. While we were talking, a police officer walked in the door. They asked if I had a gun on the property and I told them no.

I asked the other guys in front of the officer, "What about the guns you guys have when you walk through this place making threats?"

One of the guys said in a calm voice, "Mr. Blackshear, we wouldn't do anything like that. Don't try to switch the story."

The officer asked the manager if this was true, and of course, he said no. He called the salesman that I had shown my gun to into the office. He was African-American.

The manager asked him, "Charles, do you ever see us bringing guns in here?"

Charles instantly said, "No."

I couldn't believe it.

"What about Mr. Blackshear?" the manager asked.

"He said he was tired of these crackers and he was going to bring his gun in here and shoot one of them," Charles lied.

My mouth dropped. The only part of his statement that was true was that I showed him my gun but I never made those statements.

The officer asked me if I wouldn't mind going outside so they could look in my car to make sure there was no gun there. They went out to my car but they didn't see anything inside the car. Then they told me to open the trunk. My heart was racing because the gun was in the trunk. They moved some stuff around, lifted up some papers, and said they didn't see a gun in there. I was stunned. I thought that maybe someone had stolen it. The officer left and the manager told me he needed me to leave the property until he got in touch with the owner. I drove home and looked in the trunk. The gun was still hidden under my cleaning towel. I knew instantly that God had protected me again.

The next day, the owner called me for a meeting. Before we began he said, "Let's pray." I was shocked when he said, "As William speaks, let me hear the truth from his heart." After we prayed, I told him everything that was taking place in the dealership. He told me, "Believe it or not, William. I believe you." While I was talking, God put in his spirit that I was telling the truth. He asked me if anyone had ever told me that I had a call on my life. I remembered what Rev. John H. Jamison had said to me nearly two years earlier.

The owner said, "William, I won't put you back in that situation by sending you back to work, but here's what I will do for you instead. I will give you a month's salary so you can get back on your feet." I couldn't believe that he was willing to do that! I was thanking God but at the same time, I was frustrated because that was the ninth job that I had lost in a year. I felt like it wasn't meant for me to live.

That night I went to Maria's house because I wanted to be around somebody. I blocked my telephone number, called my friend, and told him to make sure my son knew that I loved him and to tell my family I was sorry. Then I just hung up the phone. I knew he couldn't call me back because he didn't have my number. I prayed that night and told God that if He was real, I needed to see it.

I went to sleep and when I woke up the next morning, I was led to turn on the television. When I turned on the television, Creflo Dollar said loudly, "YOU, laying in that bed! The reason you lost nine jobs in a year is because you won't answer your call!" I could not believe what I was hearing! By the time I could speak, he was saying, "Now let's get back to today's message." I couldn't explain it. I got on my knees and prayed to God. I promised Him I was going to serve Him and live right. He didn't have to worry about me smoking, doping, or drinking ever again.

Later, I called the station to order the CDs. When they arrived weeks later, I listened to each CD in the series, but Creflo Dollar's message to me wasn't there. I knew then that God used that message to speak to me because He knew I was seriously considering ending my life.

After spending all morning with God, I called Maria that afternoon and I told her that I had to end our relationship. I had to answer my call and get closer to God. I believed I was being obedient to what God wanted me to do.

I didn't know what church to go to but I didn't feel I should go to the same church where she was going because I didn't want to run into her. I fasted and repented and I was led to a new church. I told Maria that she had to trust me and let me get closer to God, and if God wanted her in my life then she would still be there. She didn't understand and got angry. She called a couple of times while I was attending church but I was so on fire for God that I didn't have the taste for her anymore. We never got back together, but the closer I came to God, the more He showed me how my behavior in my relationship with Maria was unacceptable. I asked God to forgive me, and I prayed that He would give me the opportunity to apologize to her one day.

• • •

I didn't find another job right away. I took a whole month off to fellowship with God. One night while I was praying my Mom called. She said she had some bad news. Before she could say it, it was in my spirit, I knew my dad had passed away. I sat on my bed and everything became quiet. I knew that the devil wanted me to throw in the towel. I was upset because I hadn't spoken to my dad for a whole year because he kept ignoring me and not calling me back, so I decided to do the same thing and I didn't call him either.

I called my sisters, who had moved down to Durham, and we drove to New York for the funeral. I talked to God and He told me that everything would be okay. I said to myself that I wouldn't cry for a man who never showed me he cared. He died having never said, "I love you" to me. I prayed and asked if my dad had ever given himself to God. That was all I cared about.

At the funeral, his best friend, Wilfred Scott, gave the eulogy. He said that my dad always talked about the regrets he had raising his kids, wishing he had done a better job. Wilfred used to say to my dad, "You need to give your life to God so he can forgive you." Then Wilfred said the unexpected. "I want to tell you that Robert called me over on Super Bowl Sunday and asked me to say the sinner's prayer with him. Then three days later, he died." When he said that, everything in my body shouted and I passed out.

When I woke up, I was lying on the couch and people were fanning me. I could hear my dad's voice saying, "William, I love you." His girlfriend was standing over me and I asked her if he ever said anything about me. She told me that he was proud of me for leaving New York to make something better of myself. He wished that he had taken me up on my offer and moved with me. That gave me peace in my spirit.

After the funeral, my sisters and I drove back to Charlotte. I didn't know how I was going to pay my rent, but I also knew I wasn't going to ask Maria. I just had to trust God. When I got home, Maria had left a note on my door saying she was sorry about my dad and to call her if I needed anything. She wished me well on my journey with God and she added a postscript: "Since you've been such a good friend and I've watched you grow, I paid your rent already." I was so thankful because I hadn't asked her to do it but God had laid it on her heart. She had received her income tax money and paid my rent. Glory to God.

I promised God I would go on a forty day fast to see what He wanted me to do and what church he wanted me to join. During this time, I got a call from my Uncle Joe in New York, the one who was heavily involved in politics. He asked me if I knew that Ms. Smith was living in Charlotte and he suggested that I call her. Her son was Byron Smith, the guy who was dating my first son's mother, Renee, when my son died. It was hard for me to call and talk to Ms. Smith because I still didn't know what really happened to my son.

When I finally called her, she was happy to hear from me and asked why I had waited so long to call her after moving to Charlotte. She asked me where I was working and I told her about my last job at the dealership. She told me she worked for Charlotte-Mecklenburg Schools and she was going to make a call to the superintendent. I was amazed that I was in my fasting and God was moving.

I went to the Superintendent's office that day but he was not there. The receptionist told me to fill out an application. There were two open positions. The first position was for a behavioral specialist and the other was for a teacher's assistant at a middle school. I applied for the one that was paying the most money, which was the behavioral specialist.

Several weeks went by and I didn't hear anything about the job, and then I got a call that the superintendent wanted to see me the next day. I went down to the school board, got off the elevator, and saw a man walking into his office. When he saw me, he asked if he could help me.

I said, "Yes, my name is Mr. Blackshear. I have an interview with the superintendent."

He said, "You're talking to him."

Then he looked me up and down and said, "My God! You're a big guy. Look at your shoulders and arms. How much weight can you lift?"

While I was unemployed I worked out, ran, and kept my body in shape, not knowing it would help me get a job. He asked what position I had applied for. I told him I'd applied for the behavioral specialist position. He told me that the position had been filled, but he said there was another position at the middle school and asked if I wanted it. I said yes. He told me to show up the next day and gave me the address. He also told me that he would send over the application so I could change it and put down the teacher's assistant position instead of the behavioral specialist job. Then he added, "There's one more thing I have to let you know. It's only paying about two hundred and thirty dollars, every two weeks after taxes." When I heard that, I was disappointed. It wasn't going to be enough for me to live comfortably and pay my bills.

While I was driving to work the next day, I was so angry with God that I started cursing at Him aloud saying, "You want me to follow you but how am I supposed to live when my rent is more than what I'm getting paid monthly?" The superintendent also told me that he was putting me in a classroom with a boy who had brought a gun with him to school and the whole school was terrified of him. When he told me about the gun, his words went in one ear and out the other. I was already used to that life.

Chapter 20

SOULED OUT

Instantly, I could see that the kids were trying me. I prayed and asked God to give me wisdom. I asked the teacher if I could speak to the class. I told them about my past, about being in a gang, and that I was there to help them. I told them I wasn't looking for anyone to be faking jacks with me (being a phony). Right away, I saw the fear in their eyes but that wasn't why I gave the speech.

As time passed, those boys gravitated toward me like I was their dad. Whatever I asked them to do, they did it. If I told them to pull up their pants, they did. If I told them to apologize to a teacher, they did. The principal called me into the office and said that she was hearing great things about me. She said there was a kid in the school that was unreachable and she wanted me to work with him, too. She told me that one of the teachers would bring him to lunch and introduce us.

I started working with him and eating lunch with him in the cafeteria. Initially he acted tough, but eventually, he looked forward to eating lunch with me. I also started going to his classes with him. When it was time for him to go to class, we walked the halls together. His teachers were impressed with his progress. Earlier that year, he had swung on one of his teachers and cursed him out. My work with him made other teachers come to me and ask if I would come to their classrooms to get their students under control. They sent kids to me who acted out. I counseled them and talked to them, and they begged me to come to their classes.

One day, a teacher came to me and told me that he had been watching me and was very pleased with the way I handled the students' behavior. He told me he was getting ready to open a group home and he wanted me to be the manager. The facility would be up and running in the summer. He also said that he had a friend with a group home that was currently open and he had told him about me. They were expecting my call.

I called the guy, had the interview, and got the job instantly. At the group home, I met a guy who told me he was going to University Church. He asked if I was a Christian and a minister. I told him I was a Christian, but I wasn't a minister.

I went from being mad at God because I wasn't making enough money, to not even caring about the money. I felt like my life had purpose. The kids looked up to me. I finally found people who accepted me for me. During my lunchtime, I played ball with them and ate with them. Often times, I met them at the ballpark after school and simply hung out with them. What they didn't know was that I was reliving my childhood. The kids told me that I was like a dad to them. They often told me that they loved me and asked me not to leave them.

At school, the boys saw me dressing differently. Sometimes I wore jeans and sneakers and sometimes I wore my suit. The kids surprised me one day and came in wearing their suits. It brought tears to my eyes. The principal sent out a memo to the entire faculty stating she was very pleased with the way I dressed. She said I took the dress code to another level and she wanted the teachers to consider dressing a little better. Some teachers were upset while other teachers were pleased. When the school year ended and it was time for the boys to graduate, the school was back on track and the principal begged me to come back to their school the following year.

That day when I got home, there was a message on my answering machine. The voice said, "Hello, Mr. Blackshear. I think we have a problem. I think someone has been using your name. We pulled your record and it says you've been arrested seven times. Can you please call us to straighten this out?" I called back that day and told her it was not a mistake. Within ten minutes, she called me back. She thanked me for the wonderful job that I had done at the middle school but told me that I could not work for CMS again.

I went to work that night at the group home and the same guy that was going to University Church came up to me and said, "I meant to tell you that you have a call on your life." He asked me to come to his church. He didn't know that I'd been fasting and asking God which church to join.

He said, "Why don't you come visit the church that one of the pastors from University Church just started. It's called New Bethel. The pastor's name is John H. Jamison." Instantly it clicked. I pulled the card out of my wallet, showed it to him, and asked if it was the same guy. He said yes and asked me how I got his card. I told him that Pastor Jamison had counseled me before my divorce and that he told me that I had a call on my life. I didn't know what it meant, but it made my spirit feel good.

I told him what happened at the school and he told me to just keep praying and believing God, but also to come to the church that Sunday. When he invited me to the church I didn't go right away. I told him I had to pray and make sure it was where God wanted me to go. I was still going to University Church but it didn't feel the same.

Finally, I visited New Bethel. They were in a recreational center and it was a little different. It wasn't a traditional church and they only had a few members. After service ended, I went up to the Pastor and showed him his card. He said he remembered me and he was glad to see me. He asked me what church I attended. I told him that I was going to University Church, however, it was not registering in my spirit anymore.

I joined New Bethel Community Church. During that time, God moved speedily. Not only did I join the church but I got a job as a group home manager making $72,000 a year. I made an impact on many troubled teens that were going in and out of group homes. I counseled them, encouraged them, and trained the staff and the owners about behaviors and how to work with children from various backgrounds. I also lived in the home so I didn't have to pay for anything. God's favor was all around me.

I attended church regularly and after a while, Pastor Jamison suggested that I attend the Ministers-In-Training (MIT) classes to become a licensed minister. I was on fire for God but it didn't take long for me to find out that even though you join the church and have a relationship with God, the devil continues to try his best to stop the growth in your life. The enemy came at me in ways I couldn't even imagine but I continued to fight the good fight of faith and I thank God that it never drove me back to gang life, drugs and alcohol, or stealing and scamming. I was no longer in the street and I felt total freedom. I received the baptism in water and as I came up, I knew I was a free man.

I had attended church for about three months when God put on my spirit that I needed to get rid of my gun. I came home from church one day and I threw the gun away. He also challenged me to get rid of everything that He didn't bless me with. He told me to trust only Him and start all over. I gave away my cars, my diamond rings and watches, my designer clothes and shoes, and all of my gators. I sold my heart to God and did exactly what He told me to do.

In return, he answered one of my most earnest prayers. I was leaving church one Sunday, and I decided to walk to the Family Dollar store. I was walking around the store, and God allowed me to run into Maria again. We were both surprised to see each other, but we made an awkward attempt at small talk. I told her that I had decided to become a minister. Before she could say anything else, I was obedient to the opportunity God had given me and I quickly said, "I'm so glad to see you. I wanted to apologize, for my actions."

By the look on her face, I could tell she didn't know what to say. Then, out of nowhere, her mother appeared from one of the aisles. She said she had heard what I said to her daughter. With tears in her eyes, she thanked me for apologizing to Maria. She said to me, "If my daughter cannot see it, let me be the one to tell you that I am amazed that you are a changed man." She asked Maria if she could see how God had worked in my life. She had no response at that time. She simply said thank you for the apology and told me the kids were doing okay. She grabbed her bags, put them in her mother's car, and proceeded to walk a couple doors down to Pizza Hut.

I walked with her and asked her, "How have you been doing?" She replied, "Fine." Then, all of a sudden, the emotions started coming back and she said, "I thank you for apologizing to me and walking with me, but you walked out of my life and left me. I have to admit, I'm still hurting and it's still upsetting." I told her that I understood and I walked away and got into my car. I was relieved that God had answered my prayers and allowed me to apologize to her.

Please hear my heart when I say that an apology does not remove the pain a woman endures when a man takes her through what Maria and I experienced during our relationship. You must protect yourself and guard your heart by taking time to get to know the person you choose to date. If he or she has survived experiences similar to mine, you *cannot* become a problem solver or a healer. Don't fool yourself. Healing must come from God.

Too often, we get in God's way, not realizing that when we don't allow God to heal someone who is still broken, we risk activating triggers of pain, rejection, and hurt. It only takes a simple word or action to set off those triggers and cause an emotional outburst. You may blame yourself and think, *what did I do wrong or what did I say wrong?* Their reactions won't make sense to you. What seems like a small thing to you, may activate a memory of hurt and rejection for them.

The outward expression of this pain may look like profanity, physical violence or the decision to end the relationship and leave you.

It may have nothing to do with you but it has everything to do with his or her internal pain. Until God comes into those areas, heals them, and teaches them how to love in a Godly and healthy way, he or she will be no good to you.

Chapter 21

BLIND LEADING THE BLIND

Before you read this chapter, it is important for me to take a moment to speak to those who are engaged to be married or desire to marry in the future, but have not yet allowed God to deliver them from the generational curses of their family bloodline.

You may be saved and on fire for God, but if the only model of marriage you have is what you observed in a dysfunctional family marriage, you are in danger of repeating the relationship patterns that you want to avoid. I was on fire for God but I was trying to have a successful marriage based on the dysfunctional model I observed in my home. Praise God, there's a solution! Proverbs 18:22 (NASB) states, "He who finds a wife finds a good thing and obtains favor from the Lord." Before you enter into a marital relationship, learn to fully submit yourself to God and do things HIS way.

• • •

Shortly after joining the church, I began dating one of the women. I didn't know that I was a prophet but when I went to Monique's house, I saw things that made me think I was going crazy. I saw visions of guys she had introduced me to and the Spirit revealed to me that they were men she was sleeping with. The thug was leaving me but God was with me.

One day, she invited me to a cookout and introduced me to one of her friends. She introduced him as her 'brother' but when he passed by he rubbed his body against her. I saw it but I convinced myself that I was just seeing things. Eventually, I got tired of her playing games with me and I dropped her.

The devil tried me with Monique, but I thank God. He blocked it. I just wanted to be married and I wanted to be loved. I didn't just want to sleep with women, I wanted a real relationship. I thought I had found the good girls in church. I didn't realize that everyone in church is there for a reason.

I met with Pastor Jamison about joining MIT. I hoped that it would help me to forget about Monique. I was on fire for God and I was excited about becoming a minister. I wanted to share my story, even though Pastor told me not to. One night in class, I told my story, including that I used to date married women. My classmates were all college educated. The minute I shared my story, they judged me. The guys didn't trust me and the women were afraid of me. They stopped inviting me to their gatherings and they shunned me.

I was miserable at the church because I didn't use wisdom and I was mad at God because he brought me to a church where no one understood me. The next time I went back to MIT class I had something to say, "Not another damn person is going to run me away from what God has for me." The room fell silent. God said that He would not allow me to be put to shame but I was miserable and I wanted to leave the class.

• • •

It didn't take long for me to find another woman. The day Teresa walked into the sanctuary, I knew that she was different from the other women. She dressed differently, she walked differently, she even spoke differently. I could see that she was a woman who was there for God . . . or so I thought.

One Sunday after service, I was talking to one of the musicians when she approached me and said, "Is God telling you anything about being with me?" Instantly, I felt that she had a Jezebel spirit and I said, "Oh my God." The Spirit told me that she was only acknowledging me because of my money. When I testified in MIT, I also told them about my job at the group home. I heard Him but I was drawn to her.

Teresa and I went out to dinner and had a great time. When I told Pastor he said, "Don't ever do it again. Before you get involved with a woman at this church, come talk to me about the situation." I felt bad because I thought we had a good time.

The following week, it was time for the church to identify leaders. Pastor picked twelve people to go on a retreat. Teresa got picked, but I didn't. She decided not to attend so she could stay at home with me. She came over and we watched movies and ate pizza.

That Sunday, I came into church first and then she came in and sat right beside me. I didn't think anyone noticed. I was there to praise God and have a relationship with Him but when it was time for the Word to come, I felt eyes on me. Monique was staring at me and I saw other people looking, too. I leaned over and told Teresa not to worry about it.

When service was over, everyone asked if she was my girlfriend and I told them no, that we were just talking. I was standing in the back of the church when Pastor and First Lady walked by and one of the fellas said, "Hey Pastor, this is Blackshear's friend," pointing at Teresa.

Pastor said, "You all need to come and talk to me," and he kept walking.

We made an appointment for two weeks later. We kept hanging out but we started arguing. I was fearful and felt that God was trying to show me that Teresa was not the one for me. I told her about it and I could see the fear on her face. She was afraid she was going to lose me, so she gave in one night and we had sex. When we were finished, she cried. She told me that she hadn't had sex for three years and that she felt connected to me. I knew we were wrong for having sex, but I still felt special.

In our meeting with Pastor, we told him about our challenges. He said, "You all need to slow down, pray, and hear from God." But . . . we didn't. We kept talking behind closed doors and eventually I told Pastor I wanted to talk to him about marriage.

He set up the conference and we met with him a few times. We discussed my personal challenges and my issues with Teresa. Pastor told us again that we needed to slow down and that we should consider taking a break from each other. As soon as he finished speaking, Teresa screamed, "You can't tell us that! God is the one who sets up relationships and marriages. That's not your job! Your job is to counsel us and marry us. God will speak to US if this is not right!"

I sat there and didn't say anything. I was stunned. I was fearful of standing up to Pastor because his temperment reminded me of my dad. Pastor sat there, let Teresa finish, and then said, "I can't counsel you any more unless you all get help."

Over the next few weeks, Teresa and I argued like cats and dogs. It seemed we had nothing in common. Our main agrument was that she thought she was better than me. She acted like I should be grateful that a woman like her would even date a man like me.

"All my men were athletic. They were at least six-foot-two," she said.

"I don't know why you think you're all that. You're not the type of woman I date anyway. I like short women with long hair," I responded.

When we argued, I got turned off. She was very controlling but so was I. After the argument, she went home and I stayed at my place.

A couple days later, she finally called. We let it go like it never happened. However, I was still frustrated and I wasn't sure I should be with her. During our argument, she said, "That's why some of that stuff happened in your past." I thought she was saying, "That's why you got molested." I never released that and I kept hate in my heart towards her but I stayed with her because she accepted me for who I was and I was afraid of being alone again.

We dated for two and a half months and then got married. First Lady called me the day before the wedding and asked me, "Is this of God?" Everything in my spirit said, "No," but I said, "Yes." I was fascinated that Teresa accepted all of my mess. Not knowing that I was supposed to get in touch with God first, I gave her all the power.

The day we got married, I knew I didn't love her. My heart was racing and thumping as I walked down the aisle. I could hear the Holy Spirit saying, *"Don't do it."* My feet almost came from under me. The Spirit was trying to stop me and I thought I would pass out. My family was there and I didn't want to let them down.

We went to the beach for our honeymoon but I was turned off and I couldn't get motivated to be with her. When we argued she said, "You're nothing." When we had sex previously she had said, "Oh, that's nothing. I've had bigger." It hurt me but I played macho. Her words were planted in my spirit and I just couldn't bring myself to have sex with her.

I left the hotel and went to the liquor store, thinking that being drunk would get me motivated. It didn't. We didn't consumate our marriage on our honeymoon. The day we were getting ready to leave she said, "God showed me why you're not turned on. You haven't been released from the light-skinned, Puerto Rican girls." It hit me like a brick because I knew it was true, but it felt like she was attacking me.

We drove back in silence while God told me that she was speaking the truth. We dated for two months and got married the third month. We did not have time to remove the idols in our hearts, so we used them as weapons. I didn't know how to go to God and ask him to change me.

• • •

Two weeks into the marriage, her mom called and asked to speak to her. Then she asked to speak to me and told me to leave the room. She said, "I prayed for you two but I'm telling you the truth. You're about to go through hell." It was confirmation.

"What did mom say?" Teresa asked.

"Nothing. We just prayed together."

We didn't make love the entire first month of our marriage, so we decided to go in for more counseling.

Pastor said, "I've never had to counsel a couple during the first month."

"You know how Blackshear is. This is all in his mind," Teresa said, and Pastor believed her.

Eventually, we had sex but it was boring. She started using her body to control me but I knew it, so I began looking elsewhere. I am a night owl and Teresa went to bed at nine o'clock. To me, that's rejection. I told her, "You should be lucky to be married to a man like me." I was full of pride.

One day while I was out looking for trouble, I found it. I met a girl in the store who wasn't my type but I liked her body. I started calling her while Teresa was sleeping and we talked for hours at a time. I even bought her a nightie and took it to her house, but while I was there her baby's father called. God intervened. I gave her the nightie and told her to use it with her boyfriend. I never saw her again.

When Teresa got the phone bill with the strange long distance number, she called the number. The girl told her that she knew me but I didn't sleep with her. Teresa said that it was still considered cheating. I disagreed. Honestly, I was still upset and I didn't care. She tried to make me feel privilieged that a woman like her would even choose me and she threw up my past to prove her point. She continued to provoke me until I screamed, "Leave me the hell alone!"

BLIND LEADING THE BLIND

She jumped up and she pushed me. I pushed her back and she hit the wall. When I walked away she said, "You just pushed the wrong person and you're going to get it!"

When the police arrived, the kids cried and said that Teresa was mean to them. She never did like the kids. She told the cops that I beat her. They checked her body for bruises and didn't find any. They removed me from the house because I was angry. I didn't like it, but my spirit was at peace.

When they released me the next day, I called Pastor and he asked me what happened. We had a counseling session scheduled for that morning and we didn't show up. I told him I went to jail because Teresa and I got into a fight. He told me to come see him after Bible Study but I told him I didn't want to come.

When I went back to the house, the owners of the group home were there. Teresa admitted to Tim and Marla that she lied and told the police that I hit her when we had only pushed each other. They told me that we had to leave.

Tim said, "Will, I don't know what happened. Before she came into your life, you were on target. You had a rapport with the kids and with me and Marla. Didn't I tell you that she wasn't the woman for you because she was too aggressive?" All I could do was hang my head because I knew he was right.

After ten days passsed, they changed the locks on the doors and we couldn't get into the house. I called Pastor and I called a few church members. No one ever called me back. With the money I had in the bank, we checked into a hotel and paid by the week. I hated myself because I had gone from the top to the bottom. I couldn't function anymore because I missed my job and I missed working with the kids.

We went to counseling again but it never got better. She used my past against me. I thought I was being punished. I thought that God would have worked on our hearts or it would be God's will for us to be together. It just didn't happen.

One day, she taunted me and we got into another physical fight. Then she said, "That's why your uncle raped you." I jumped on her and started pounding her on the back. She got up and said, "You're gonna pay for that." I knew she was right.

Just because I was off the street, it didn't mean that some of my behaviors didn't follow me. I didn't allow God to clean up my DNA. I wasn't doing what I did in the streets but there were still behaviors in me. I didn't know how to be a man, let alone be a spiritual man. Later, her friends showed up at our place to get her stuff. They tried to jump me but I kicked them out.

We met with Pastor again and she made me look like the devil. I got up, left, and walked home the ten miles. I left my car in the parking lot. I was angry with God and I was angry with Pastor for not exposing her. I was reaping what I sowed.

• • •

In May, Teresa went out of town to a women's conference. I was so hurt that I went back to my old ways. I missed my old girlfriends and I even called Susan but I was unable to reach her. I hooked up with someone I'd met when I was working in the school system and I cheated on my wife.

Two months later, I told Teresa about the cheating and I told her that I wanted to be free. We went to counseling again and I had to go through a high level of accountability. We went through counseling for two years, until Pastor said he couldn't do it anymore.

When we went to the new counselor, Teresa told him the truth: She didn't like me and she didn't like Pastor because of his temperment, and she took it out on me. Our counselor advised us to begin sleeping in separate rooms. I slept in the bedroom and she slept in the living room and had access to the kitchen. We had to respect each other's space. I even had to ask her if I could go into the kitchen. Some nights, she cooked dinner for herself and I would go back into the bedroom and cry. I was miserable.

One night, while she was out, the enemy started talking to me . . . and I listened. I hung myself from the light fixture in the living room. As I felt my spirit leaving me, I was at peace. I felt the sweat and urine pouring from my body and I knew I was almost done. Then all of a sudden, the rope broke. When I came to, there were several police officers around me and Pastor was there. When Teresa came home and found me, she had called 911 and then she called Pastor Jamison.

We went through another round of counseling but nothing changed. In one of my individual sessions, the counselor told me to be prepared because Teresa was going to leave me. I had a dream that God told me to look on a table and I would find papers. When I woke up, I looked on the hall table and I saw her resume. It was confirmation. I knew she was going to leave me.

The next day, I told her that she didn't have to pay anymore bills. She left the house, went shopping, and bought clothes. Over the next few weeks, I bought her dinner and gifts and kept being kind to her. God gave her time to change, but she didn't. She started dressing inappropriately at work and they cut back her hours. Boils came up all over her body and the church was afraid of her. I prayed for God to slow my money down so she wouldn't want to stay.

One day, she grabbed a butcher knife, held it to my neck, and said in a voice I'd never heard before, "I will slice your head off," and then she turned the knife into my neck. Another time, she sliced me with the four-karat ring I'd bought for her. Another time, she busted a broomstick on the counter and tried to come at me with it. I was nice to her through all of it. I prayed to God that if it was His will, she would leave me.

I knew that the devil was assigned to kill me but I wouldn't let the spirit within her succeed. She left with a car and that was it. I wished her well.

I knew that my disobedience about marrying too quickly had caused the enemy to attempt to destroy my character and kill me.

In spite of our marital issues, I appreciated her coming into my life. Our marriage forced me to get closer to God. Being with Teresa helped me to have a deep and intimate relationship with Him.

I wish it could have worked out, but what do you do when you're the blind one trying to lead someone else, while everything is still dark in your own world?

One day, I received a letter from her apologizing for her actions during the marriage. Later, she called and we forgave each other and we were able to share a laugh. That was the last time we spoke. It was the end of our season together and we went our separate ways.

A few months later, I decided to follow my vision of operating my own group home. A minister at the church blessed me with a house to start my business. He allowed me to have the house rent-free for six months. I knew that God was blessing me for staying faithful after my wife and I split up. I hadn't seen or touched a woman for over a year. It would seem as if my strength, power and my anointing was growing stronger through God. My divorce continued to draw me closer to God and caused me to have a love hunger for Him through praising, worshiping and serving God wholeheartedly.

The group home was coming along well when the devil surprised me with another major struggle . . . a woman. She was very attractive and looked like a model. The devil always knew how to distract me. She joined the youth ministry where I served. We became friends and built a relationship over the course of several conversations. There was an instant connection.

One Sunday, she passed by Pastor and me in the hallway. Pastor immediately warned me to be careful. He didn't know that I was already involved with Regina.

I allowed her to help me operate the group home. It appeared as though we were building a strong friendship together. Eventually, we became sexually involved, which of course, made me draw closer to her. God continued to warn me in my spirit that I needed

BLIND LEADING THE BLIND

to move away from her, but I hardened my heart and continued to do my own thing.

As our relationship progressed and Pastor preached, I would be convicted during service by the message. Afterwards, Regina and I would decide to back off from seeing each other for a while, but then we would give in to the temptation and resume spending time together again. After a while, I realized that I was sinking deep into sin with her.

I called Pastor one Monday morning and confessed to him that our relationship had been going on for two months. He told me that we needed to see him on Tuesday after Bible Study. When we met with him, he told us that our relationship was not of God and instructed us to stop seeing each other immediately. I disobeyed the instruction.

When Pastor found out that I was still reaching out to her, he was upset. He asked me, "Didn't I give you a directive and tell you to leave her alone?" Because of my disobedience, he sat me down and put me on sabbatical. He told me to call every ministry that I served in and tell them that I was relieved from all of my duties. I loved to serve and leaving my ministries left me miserable and hurting.

During my sabbatical, God told me that Regina was going to bring a guy to church but I didn't know if that was my mind speaking or God. However, the following Sunday, as I pulled into the church parking lot, she was pulling up with a guy in her car. It had only been about a month since we were last together. I prayed to God and asked Him, *what should I do?* God told me to keep praising Him.

During the service when we welcomed visitors, I rushed to the guy and thanked him for coming to the church. Then I went back to my seat and continued to praise God and enjoy the service. When I left church that day, I had peace. God would later reveal to me that Regina had her own issues with men. I was caught in the lap of Delilah and I didn't even know it. She had found my strength and taken it from me.

Eventually, I lost the group home as a result of my disobedience to God. I tried to look for another job but the only job I found was at a pizza place. I went from working for a profitable organization that brought in over two hundred thousand dollars a year to making a little more than six dollars an hour as a pizza delivery driver. I learned a hard lesson about being obedient to God. I knew in my spirit God allowed me to work at the pizza place so that I may be humbled and fully return back to Him.

I moved into a one-bedroom apartment with a roommate. I had to sleep on the floor. My roommate was still on drugs. When I came home from work, he was often in the apartment getting high. I was angry that I put myself in that position but through it all, I kept my devotion to God. I also kept my ministry in my heart and I continued to serve people. I even ministered to people on my job and one of my coworkers turned his life over to God. It seemed like the minute he got saved, a new job opened up to me.

Chapter 22

FREE

"If the Son therefore shall make you free, ye shall be free indeed"

(John8:36 KJV)

As I continued my sabbatical, Pastor Jamison assigned me to an accountability partner. He told me, "I want you to call Minister Bill morning, noon, and night!" Pastor didn't know that Bill was controlling and manipulative. He was actually the one who had shared the reason for my sabbatical with the other ministers. I was living out the story of Saul and David. It seemed the more I tried to be nice to Minister Bill, the more he would throw spears at me. He made the season of my sabbatical very difficult for me because he didn't like me so he treated me with cruelty. When Pastor showed me favor, Bill attacked me. But I stayed humble and did everything he told me to do when I would call him. The people in the church attacked me, too, and distanced themselves from me. I felt rejected by several ministers in the church. But through it all I continued to keep my relationship with God, always praising and worshipping Him.

At the end of that season, I got back on track and began serving on ministries again. All I would do is focus on strengthening my relationship with God, serve faithfully on the ministries, and live a wholesome life in the church. The Bible says "vengeance is mine" and within four months of my return to serving on ministries,

Minister Bill was released from all of his ministerial duties for character issues he displayed himself regarding women. The very minister who had attacked me several times, and was responsible for holding me accountable during my season, could not serve out his own sabbatical and wound up leaving the church. At that time, I was asked to take over one of the ministries for which he previously served as leader, and I became co-leader of the intercessory prayer ministry. I had been free from any issues with women for the past four years. My prayer life, along with the intercessory prayer ministry grew stronger. Pastor allowed me to speak into others' lives as God gave me the unction during intercessory prayer gatherings we had at the church each week. I later found out that this was another gift from God that He was working through me. As I continued to grow closer to God and in the gift He had given me, the devil was quickly on the move once again.

A woman named Jackie joined the intercessory prayer team. I thought nothing about it at the time, when she joined the ministry, but I would notice she was being overly expressive when she would pray and sing. For some reason, I began to sense in my spirit she was trying to impress me. But I wasn't moved as I was still guarding my heart. But one day while walking to my car, Jackie was also leaving the church. She called me over to her car and asked, "Hey, what's your name again?" I replied to her, "Now, come on. You know my name." She giggled, and then said with a smile, "I just wanted to tell you I enjoyed your prayer. You pray with a lot of power". She expressed how she was moved when I would share prophesy with people. She also told me that if God ever lays anything on my heart about her, please don't hesitate to call, and she reached out her hand to give me a piece of paper with her phone number written on it. I hesitated for a moment, but I took her number.

We started calling each other but we didn't talk about anything spiritual or church related. Our conversation was more about how she could help me with my job by completing administrative tasks for me. We continued to connect on the phone, but I still had no desire or feelings for her. I mentioned to her one time on the phone she needs a covering being down here in Charlotte by herself. I felt my old ways slipping back in, but thought I could control it, and not allow things to go too far. She asked me if it was okay for us to be talking on the phone and for me to be praying for her. I told her it wasn't a problem and Pastor wouldn't mind. That lie was the first way I allowed the devil a foothold to creep back in. I knew Pastor would mind, but at this time she was being a benefit in my life by helping me with those tasks at work I found difficult. During some of our conversations, she would ask me to come over. I knew I was not willing to cross boundaries in that way so I would reject her and tell her no. I really was trying to keep myself from any tempting situations that could lead to sexual activity. We remained friends but we argued often because she had similar character traits like my ex-wife. She tried to control me and it pushed my buttons. This also made it very easy for me not to get involved with her sexually.

• • •

At the end of the year, I got sick and was rushed to the hospital, where I was diagnosed with diabetes. While I was there, Jackie called and I told her what the doctor had told me. When I was released from the hospital, I became depressed and I didn't talk to anyone for several days. Then one night the phone rang. It was Jackie. She called me at the right time saying, "I cooked some wheat noodles and turkeyburgers. You want to come over?" That was her way of letting me know she had found a meal appropriate for a diabetic. I was moved by her thoughtfulness. I went to see her, we ate dinner, and then we had sex. In the middle of our escapade, she asked me to stop. It was two o'clock in the morning so I got dressed and got ready to leave. Then she asked me to stay. She wanted to make sure that even if she wasn't sleeping with me that I wasn't going to leave her. It worked and I stayed until four o'clock in the morning.

Over the next few weeks, Jackie and her daughter came to my house and I spent time with them. I even took her daughter to the park to play and it felt like we were becoming a family . . . until Jackie started missing her ex-boyfriends. She started dogging me out and I was crushed. Once again, my dreams of having a happy family were shattered. I couldn't pray. I couldn't function in my ministerial duties. I was miserable.

I thought I had a family but then Jackie stopped returning my calls. After three months of not hearing from her, I was done with her. When I saw her and she spoke to me, I ignored her. Until one day I was standing outside of Pastor's office and one of the armor bearers said that Pastor wanted to see me after service. Jackie walked by with another girl and instanly I knew it had something to do with her.

After service, I went to Pastor Jamison's office and he told the armor bearer, "Go get that girl." First Lady was there with him and she said, "We know this is not like you or something you would do, but we need an explanation." Then she told Jackie to tell her story. Jackie lowered her head and tried to force herself to cry, then she looked up and said, "You raped me."

I couldn't believe what I'd just heard. I was furious. I immediately defended myself and asked Pastor, "If I raped her, why did she let her daughter stay at my house? If I raped her, why did she let me take her daugher to the park?"

I continued to confess the truth about what happened between Jackie and me. When I was done, I looked up, and I could see the look on First Lady's face. Her eyes were glossy. I could see that she was devastated by her disappointment in me. I had let her down.

Pastor called me the next day to encourage me. He told me that God still had a plan for me and I just needed to work through the process. He said, "The higher up you go, the enemy will continue to try and kill you. You have to wait until God sends you the woman that *He* has for you."

I continued attending church. Every time I saw Jackie, I was amazed that she had the audacity to speak. She kept her voice low and thought that no one else could hear her, but one day, another member of the church heard her and warned me to be careful. I immediately reported this to First Lady because Jackie was accountable to her. First Lady told me to use wisdom.

One Sunday Pastor Jamison preached a powerful message about how God rewards the unjust. I started shouting and praising God because I knew that God was telling me that even though I had been lied on and talked about, He would still reward me.

To my surprise, after service was over, Jackie asked if she could speak with me. She said, "I know you don't trust me but I have to get this out of my spirit. I'm sorry for lying about you and destroying your character. I was very interested in you and my daughter still talks about how well you treated her. Believe it or not, I believe I had to go through this because it helped me to be set free and be delivered from my dysfunctional ways. I wish I could take back how I treated you but I can't. Can you please find it in your heart to forgive me?"

I stood there in amazement. I was numb. I was filled with happiness, sadness, and confusion, but I said, "I do forgive you." Jackie thanked me and left the sanctuary.

I called Pastor and First Lady that evening and told them that a weight had been lifted off my shoulders because Jackie finally approached me and apologized.

God allowed Pastor and First Lady to remove themselves from me so I could grow closer to God. Many of the church members turned their backs on me and I no longer trusted them. This was part of God's plan so that I could focus all of my attention on Him and not on people. Often we wonder why God allows people to turn on us, but my greatest test was learning to continue to love God's people in spite of how I felt. One of the ministers told everyone who joined the church about me. She tore me down behind my back. It hurt me and it killed my spirit. The fire in me went out.

The first time I planned my demise, I was at the church. I was upset and I just wanted to get out of there, go home, and end it all. I was walking down the hallway and one of the ministers on staff stopped me. She told me that whatever was wrong, God was going to make it right. I thanked God for blocking the enemy's plan.

The second time I planned my demise, I was at church again. I was on my way out when one of the members stopped me. We had a brief conversation and it was enough to make me change my mind. I thank God that He didn't allow me to do it. The devil had followed me to church. Don't think that just because you're saved the devil won't follow you. He tried to finish me off but God had other plans.

• • •

The following year, Pastor finally restored me as an armor bearer. It had been a year since I dated a woman. During my sabbatical, there was one friend who remained in my corner. We had a previous friendship to see if God would link us for marriage but that never happened. Carissa lied to me about going back to a male friend with whom she was involved, even after Pastor told her to leave him alone because the relationship was not from God for various reasons.

One Saturday afternoon, the day before Father's Day, I told her I was going to take a nap and she said that she would take a nap also. I awakened two hours later and called her. I couldn't reach her for several hours. When she finally answered, she said she couldn't sleep, so she got up and went to the mall. Then, the call ended suddenly. I felt in my spirit that it was a trick and she never planned to take a nap. She just wanted me to be asleep for reasons I didn't know at the time but would later be revealed to me. I tried to call her back, but I couldn't reach her. The spirit told me that her phone was turned off.

She contacted me an hour later and when I asked her what happened, she told me her phone battery had died while she was out shopping. The spirit told me that something was not right about her story, but I had no proof. So, all I could do was pray, wait, and let God reveal the truth.

About a month later on a Sunday afternoon, she called me after church and said she felt convicted and had to confess something. She began to admit the truth about why I couldn't reach her that day she went shopping. She said her phone had died because she was talking on the phone for over an hour with the guy she was involved with before me. She said she just wanted to wish him Happy Father's Day. She started to cry and tried to explain how guilty and ashamed she felt for going backwards. We remained friends but not with the possibility of moving beyond a friendship. After receiving spiritual advice, I was told to remain friends with her but to give her time to grow in her areas of weakness and not allow her to have a front row seat in my life. When I explained this to Carissa, she agreed.

During our friendship, issues arose with her daughter. Her daughter didn't like me and wouldn't speak to me at church. As we discussed the issues with her daughter, I realized that we had different philosophies about raising children. Her daughter was fourteen and she was allowed to do things that I didn't think she should be able to do at that age.

As Carissa and I continued talking, I realized that if there was any possibility of us moving forward, we had to work out the issues with her daughter. I decided that it was time for me to completely remove myself from her life so that she could work with her daughter and prepare her for the possibility of us moving forward. I thought that the best way to accomplish this was without me in her life. Carissa called me and asked why I would leave her after seven months. I told her that I didn't want to come between her and her daughter. She hung up on me but she called me the next day to apologize. She asked me if my decision had anything to do with the other man. I said no. I needed to continue to work on my own issues. We talked about reconnecting after she worked out the issues with her daughter. It was important to me that she re-establish a healthy parent-child relationship with boundaries instead of what seemed to be a friend-to-friend relationship between her and her daughter. We spoke in passing when we saw each other at church, but I felt emotionless when I saw her. After helping her overcome many of her struggles, my heart was hardened and I felt worn out.

During the next seven months that followed, God allowed me to see how He was moving in her life. I watched her grow closer to God and He elevated her in the ministry. She became First Lady's assistant and a fellow armor bearer. When she became an armor bearer, I congratulated her. She said to me, this was all because of the work that you allowed God to do in me. She thanked me for allowing God to use me to make her better. Although her words should have impacted me, they had no effect didn't because my heart was still hardened. As time went by, it seemed as if everything was getting back to normal. On my birthday, I received a text message from her saying simply, "Happy Birthday". I text her back and said "Thank you. How have you been doing?" After that, we started the conversations back up here and there with texts and short phone calls to each other. We started working toward being friends once again. This went on for about two months.

Then one day, First Lady called me and asked me to pick up lunch for her. On my way to her house, I passed Carissa in traffic. I waved to her and kept going. When I arrived at First Lady's house, she told me that she was hungry and told me to go straight to the restaurant without delay. When I pulled up to the restaurant, I saw Carissa through the window. I looked closer and saw her having lunch with Tom, a member of the church. They were laughing and smiling and having a really good time. I was stunned and I immediately called First Lady and asked her if she knew about Carissa and Tom having lunch together. She didn't know what I was talking about but she hung up and called Carissa. A few minutes later, First Lady called me back and told me that she spoke with Carissa and set up a meeting with her.

This was me and Carissa's second attempt at having a friendship. Pastor advised me to take some time and seek God for guidance. I agreed but I was angry. I didn't call or see Carissa for a month. Then one Sunday, I saw another minister with his arms around her. I was too angry to respond. A couple months later, she called to tell me that she was pregnant by the same minister I saw her with. It was the worst feeling in the world to watch the woman I deeply cared for carrying another man's child inside of her. It killed my spirit.

For two years, I was angry and withdrawn. I removed myself from my ministerial duties and from the prayer rotation and I shut down. I didn't speak to her the entire two years.

Eventually, I saw her and the baby. I called her and told her my true feelings. I told her that I only acted like she didn't exist because of my anger. I prayed with her and wished her well. I would later bless her financially for her son.

I'm glad I'd forgiven her and released her. I finally allowed God to set me free from using women as a drug of choice. I realized whenever I allowed women to hurt me, all I needed to replace the pain was God. After several years of being free, I finally waited on God, and He sent me the woman He had for me.

Through God's grace, sound biblical teaching, and Pastor and First Lady's love for me, I reached a place where I remained free. I have exchanged my ways for God's ways and His grace continues to sustain me to this day.

Chapter 23

AN OPEN LETTER

If your child or someone you know exhibits behaviors of possible physical, emotional, sexual, or substance abuse, please talk to them. Take the time to ask them the crucial question: WHY? When I did things that people didn't understand, no one asked me WHY. They judged me and said I was bad. The answer to the WHY that no one cared to ask was that I was hiding the pain of being molested as a young child. I was hiding the pain of being hated by my dad and of being shunned by my family. So I did the best I could do to raise myself, whether that was stealing, robbing, gang banging or selling drugs.

We see our kids today wearing saggy pants, gang banging, and smoking weed, but I bet if you sat down and talked to them and asked them WHY they do it, they would tell you that they are scared. They are scared to tell you that they have been molested. They are scared to tell you that nobody loved them. They are scared to tell you about their fears of being judged by everyone and they are scared to tell you about their innermost thoughts that keep them up every night.

Studies show that a family member or a family friend is most likely to molest a child. Be very careful about who you allow your children to spend time with and who you allow into your home. All Satan needs is a crack to get into your home and into your child. When you are playing sexual content on your television or exhibiting inappropriate sexual behavior, you have invited the spirit of lust into your home. Be careful about what you allow your children to see with the eye gate. The enemy will use anything and anyone to get to your children—even you.

Be careful not to show favoritism to your children because God loves us all the same. When you favor one child over another, you allow the spirit of anger into your home. If your child does not have your attention, he or she may begin seeking attention from someone else and become vulnerable to various types of abuse.

Be thoughtful about the words you speak. The power of life and death are in the tongue. Speak positive, loving words to your children. This will create positive thoughts in them and their thoughts and actions will reflect this positivity. Your words can either build them up or destroy them.

Believe in your child's dreams, even if you don't agree with them or understand them. Dreams are a gift from God. Encourage your child to have a relationship with God so that he or she can hear from Him and understand what He is saying. Even if your child grows older and leaves the church, there will be a spiritual foundation to return to.

If you need help for your child, help for a loved one, or assistance with finding the path to your own healing, please see the Resources section for a list of organizations that can help you find healing and peace.

God bless you.

–William

AFTERWORD

.

Two movies have inspired me: *Radio* and *Antoine Fischer*. They told Radio that he would never be anything because of his low IQ. I, too, was called dumb, stupid, and ignorant by my family members and by my teachers. Fortunately, I realized that the words people say don't make you who you are. What makes you special is your heart.

Antoine Fisher inspired me by helping me realize that I may have been raped and molested, but just like him, I overcame my adversities, devastation, shame, and humiliation. Things happen in life. These things can lead to hopelessness, despair, depression, and loneliness. However, if you put your trust in God and in His Word, you will find that His Word is true. We can do all things through Christ who strengthens us.[9]

I thank God that He came into my life and showed me that I am somebody through Him. He also gave me a vision. Through my consulting firm, *Restoration Consulting, LLC*, I have facilitated workshops for government agencies and businesses for several years. I also founded *Project Restoration, Inc.*, a nonprofit 501(c)(3) organization that helps abused and neglected children. Through this organization, we teach children how to overcome adversities. We teach them how to turn negative experiences into positive outcomes by letting go of the addictions that mask the pain and the rejection of their pasts.

It is 2013, and I can say that I've been clean from the street life, gang life, drug dealing, and addiction for over seventeen years. I've been free from white-collar crime for over twelve years. I am a licensed minister and I serve with our youth ministry to help single mothers with their sons. I have also worked in the mental health field with children and adults for the past twelve years. God has allowed me to see many of the teenagers that I have worked with continue their education in college or join the military. Some have returned to me and shared that because God sent me into their lives, they became better people.

After teaching and volunteering with the Sheriff's Department, we have formed a partnership to make our community a safer place by restoring hope in inmates with love, peace, and joy. *Project Restoration, Inc.* works with recently released youth offenders to help them acclimatize into the community and refrain from drugs, alcohol, and gang life. We teach our teenage boys that even though they may have been incarcerated, their lives are not wasted and life is not over for them. By following a specific curriculum, we teach interviewing skills, how to obtain and maintain employment, and other important social skills.

I am grateful to the Charlotte Mecklenburg Public Library for allowing me to use their facilities to help start our program. One of our goals is to buy our own facility where we can support recently released youth offenders and runaways who look to crime because they don't have anywhere else to go. The vision includes providing housing, food, clothing, and counseling. Please visit *www.projectrestorationinc.us* for information on how you can invest in our work.

I travel as a motivational speaker and I am a licensed foster parent. I volunteer my services with the Charlotte Mecklenburg Police Department. I've worked inside Charlotte Mecklenburg Schools and with the McLeod Center, a substance abuse treatment facility. As a minister, I visit the sick and shut in and I have taken on the responsibility of being a Dad to boys in the community that come from single parent homes.

Despite my early academic challenges, having a low IQ as a child, and being diagnosed with dyslexia at an early age, I became a Certified Peer Support Specialist in mental health, substance abuse, and developmental disabilities through the University of North Carolina Chapel Hill.

For the past seventeen years, I have studied and done extensive research in order to understand my multifaceted life. I can recognize and diagnose symptoms of post traumatic stress disorder (PTSD), bipolar disorder, schizophrenia, paranoia, depression, and many other mental and behavioral issues because I have lived with them. Through my experiences in the school system, criminal justice system, and the work I do through *Project Restoration Inc.*, I have helped people to discover their issues, counseled them, prayed with them, and when necessary, referred them to a professional for additional assistance.

I understand that the world tells you that you must have a degree to provide a diagnosis or understand behavioral and mental health issues; however, it doesn't take a degree to recognize the warning signs and to help others understand what they are dealing with. I gained my experience by living through hell and I share my lessons and wisdom with those who are seeking His grace.

God's grace has been a blessing in my life. He delivered me from alcohol, drugs, gang life, low self-esteem, addiction, academic challenges, and abuse. I thank God that I never had to take medication or attend a twelve-step program.

God delivers everyone differently. My deliverance came from my dependency on God and my prayer life with Him. He did it for me and He can do it for you.

REFERENCES

1. Jeremiah 1:5 (NIV) – Before I formed you in the womb I knew you, before you were born I set you apart; I appointed you as a prophet to the nations.
2. John 10:10 (NIV) – The thief comes only to steal and kill and destroy; I have come that they may have life, and have it to the full.
3. Isaiah 26:3 (NIV) – You will keep in perfect peace those whose minds are steadfast, because they trust in you.
4. Deuteronomy 31:6 (NIV) – Be strong and courageous. Do not be afraid or terrified because of them, for the LORD your God goes with you; he will never leave you nor forsake you.
5. Genesis 19:26 (NIV) – But Lot's wife looked back, and she became a pillar of salt.
6. Deuteronomy 31:6 (NIV) – Be strong and courageous. Do not be afraid or terrified because of them, for the LORD your God goes with you; he will never leave you nor forsake you.
7. Proverbs 26:11 (NIV) – As a dog returns to its vomit, so fools repeat their folly.
8. 1 Corinthians 1:27 (NASB) – But God has chosen the foolish things of the world to shame the wise, and God has chosen the weak things of the world to shame the things which are strong
9. Philippians 4:13 (NKJV) I can do all things through Christ who strengthens me.

ABOUT THE AUTHOR

William M. Blackshear is the Founder and President of *Restoration Consulting, LLC.* He travels as a motivational speaker and supports youth and families by restoring stability to their family relationships. He has appeared on television and radio to share his testimony and teach others how to overcome adversity using his proven successful curriculum, *Nine Steps to Recovery. Restoration Consulting, LLC* provides support for individuals, groups, and families who are seeking to prepare youth to be good citizens in their community.

William is also the founder of *Project Restoration, Inc.*, a nonprofit organization with the mission to restore joy, hope, love, and peace to youth. The organization supports mentorship of young men by equipping them with the behavioral, social, and academic skills required to be successful and build their self-esteem.

He is also a Certified Peer Support Specialist (University of North Carolina at Chapel Hill). He specializes in assisting others with overcoming substance abuse addictions, alcoholism, and other social abuses. He has over twenty years of experience working with both youth and adults with mental health challenges, developmental disabilities, substance abuse addictions, and social behavior issues.

William accepted his call to ministry in 2000. He is a licensed minister and a Lay Counselor (American Association of Christian Counselors). He developed his passion for developing young men through his work with the Charlotte-Mecklenburg Sheriff's Department and the McLeod Center, located in Charlotte, NC.

William loves the Lord and is grateful for access to the keys that God promised, which allowed healing and peace within. Through it all, William stands firm on God's word.

If you would like to request William M. Blackshear to speak at your church, school, or organization, please call (704) 840-7894 or send an email to info@projectrestorationinc.us.

Restoration Consulting, LLC
Southpark Towers
6000 Fairview Road, Suite 1200
Charlotte, NC 28210

Project Restoration, Inc
PO Box 690248
Charlotte, NC 28227
www.projectrestorationinc.us

RESOURCES

The following resources are provided for parents, caregivers, and survivors of any type of abuse. If you are dealing with abuse or are helping someone to recover, please use these resources or seek additional help from a licensed professional. God bless you.

Project Restoration, Inc.

Founded by William M. Blackshear, *Project Restoration, Inc.* is a non-profit organization designed to serve youth and families who have been hurt and/or abused and are now looking to restore their soul to life. We provide the necessary tools to develop a spiritual relationship with God. Clients learn to live on purpose according to God's plan, by living in peace, receiving love, and absorbing happiness. *Project Restoration, Inc.* works with recently released youth offenders to help them acclimate into the community and refrain from drugs, alcohol, and gang life. We teach our young men that even though they may have been incarcerated, their lives are not wasted and life is not over for them. By following a specific curriculum, we teach interviewing skills, how to obtain and maintain employment, and other important social skills. For more information, visit www.projectrestorationinc.us

Restoration Consulting, LLC

Restoration Consulting, LLC is an extension of *Project Restoration, Inc.*, which offers additional training, motivational speaking, and support groups for individuals and corporate organizations. *Restoration Consulting, LLC* opens the door for a more in-depth discussion for large or small group sessions on child abuse and neglect. We believe that our youth need guidance and understanding that will allow them to redirect their learned behavior. Many youth feel they have failed other people as well as themselves. *Restoration Consulting, LLC* has the resources and experience to deliver positive results using William M. Blackshear's proven curriculum guide.

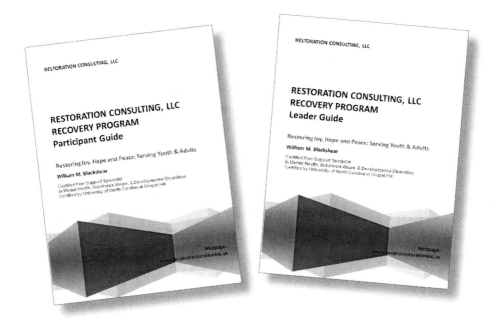

"Project Restoration, Inc has made a difference in the lives of many men and women over the past fifteen years and is building tremendous community support."

– Keith Cradle, Mecklenburg County Sheriff's Office

Adult Survivors of Child Abuse (ASCA^{SM})

http://www.ascasupport.org/

Adult Survivors of Child Abuse (ASCA ^{SM}) is an international self-help support group program designed specifically for adult survivors of neglect, physical, sexual, and/or emotional abuse. The ASCA ^{SM} program offers:

- Community based self-help support groups
- Provider based self-help support groups
- Web based self-help support groups
- Survivor to Thriver workbooks

Survivors Of Incest Anonymous

http://www.siawso.org/

SIA empowers those who have survived childhood sexual abuse (who are not abusing any child), who want to become survivors and thrivers. Using our experience, strength, and hope, we do this by:

Offering referrals to SIA self-help, support groups

Providing information to start SIA groups, intergroups, and national service offices

Creating and distributing SIA information tools (literature, newsletter, electronic media)

Offering a speakers' bureau

Guiding SIA's public information efforts worldwide

National Substance Abuse Index

http://nationalsubstanceabuseindex.org/

National Substance Addiction Treatment Hotline – 877-340-0184

National Substance Abuse Index provides a centralized, comprehensive, and easy-to-use directory for the full spectrum of resources related to dealing with alcoholism and drug addiction.

Here we provide the most up-to-date information and help with drug problems such as meth, cocaine, heroin, marijuana, club drugs, and alcohol use and abuse. We help with drug prevention, drug and alcohol rehab, and addiction recovery.

Alcoholics Anonymous

http://aa.org/

Alcoholics Anonymous® is a fellowship of men and women who share their experience, strength, and hope with each other, that they may solve their common problem and help others to recover from alcoholism. The only requirement for membership is a desire to stop drinking.

National Suicide Prevention Lifeline

1-800-273-TALK (8255)

http://www.suicidepreventionlifeline.org/
The National Suicide Prevention Lifeline provides free and confidential emotional support to people in suicidal crisis or emotional distress 24 hours a day, 7 days a week. Since its inception, the Lifeline has engaged in a variety of initiatives to improve crisis services and advance suicide prevention.

National Domestic Violence Hotline

800-799-SAFE (7233)

http://www.thehotline.org/
The National Domestic Violence Hotline creates access by providing 24-hour support through advocacy, safety planning, resources, and providing hope to everyone affected by domestic violence.

RAINN (Rape, Abuse, and Incest National Network)

800-656-HOPE (4673)

http://www.rainn.org/

RAINN (Rape, Abuse & Incest National Network) is the nation's largest anti-sexual violence organization and was named one of "America's 100 Best Charities" by Worth magazine. RAINN carries out programs to prevent sexual violence, help victims, and ensure that rapists are brought to justice.

Among its programs, RAINN created and operates the National Sexual Assault Hotline (800-656-HOPE) and online.rainn.org, an online helpline, in partnership with more than 1,100 local rape crisis centers across the country. This nationwide partnership provides victims of sexual assault with free, confidential services around the clock. The hotline has helped more than 1.5 million people since it began in 1994.

They also operate the DoD Safe Helpline (www.safehelpline.org) for the Department of Defense.

CPSIA information can be obtained at www.ICGtesting.com
Printed in the USA
BVOW08s1855220713

326637BV00015B/270/P